Seeking Jesus:

STEPPING INTO A LIFE OF BOLD SURRENDER, FREEDOM, AND DEEP JOY

JASON HOMAN & CLAUDINE BROUSSARD

F|P
FORWARD PUBLISHING

Seeking Jesus: Stepping Into a Life of Bold Surrender, Freedom, and Deep Joy

Copyright © 2017 Jason Homan.

All rights reserved. No part of this book may be reproduced or transmitted in any form or by any means without written permission of the author.

All Scripture quotations, unless otherwise specified, are taken from the King James Version.

FORWARD PUBLISHING
www.forwardpublishing.ca
Sydney Mines, Nova Scotia, Canada

DEDICATION

FROM CLAUDINE:
*To my parents, Claude & Nicole Broussard.
Thank you for instilling in me a love for music,
a love for words, and a love for Jesus.
I am so blessed to be your daughter.*

TABLE OF CONTENTS

Chapter 1	He Sought Us First	7
Chapter 2	Preparing Our Hearts to Seek Him	13
Chapter 3	The Four Circles	23
Chapter 4	Seeking Him in Prayer	35
Chapter 5	Seeking Him in Bible Study	43
Chapter 6	Scripture Memory	51
Chapter 7	Seeking Him in Meditation	57
Chapter 8	Obedience: The Test of Love	65
Chapter 9	Blessed Are the Pure in Heart	73
Chapter 10	Seeking Him in the Everyday	81
Chapter 11	Seeking His Guidance	91
Chapter 12	Seeking Him Through Discipline	101
Chapter 13	The Joy of Seeking Him	107

CHAPTER 1

He Sought Us First

From the very first moment he saw her, he loved her ardently. She was beautiful, precious, and vulnerable. A spark of hope kindled in his heart that, someday, she might accept his love. Yet there were great obstacles, high walls of division that separated the two. However, he was not at all daunted by the difficulty of the path. He labored for long, quiet years, never trying to gain attention or approval. And the years seemed but a few days, because of the love he had for her.

Patiently, he waited for the right moment to seek her hand. At last, all was in order. He earnestly pursued his beloved, calling her to come away with him. He invited her to a feast he prepared with his own hands. He offered her his name, his protection, and his love. The very best he had to offer was laid at her feet. Yet she rejected him.

"I am far too busy," she said, "Maybe later...or next week." But later never arrived, and she missed many joys that could have been. Heartsick, he poured out his heart in letter after letter of tender lines. But she only glanced through them and never bothered to reply. In truth, she was lonely. If only she had someone who would love her faithfully, hold her when life hurt, and fill the empty spaces of her heart. Her culture taught her that she would be satisfied in other ways. She didn't need mere love to be satisfied. If she chased career promotion, wealth, and a position of influence in her circle, then she would be completely fulfilled. Of course, she also needed to dress the right way, talk the right way, and think the right way. (That is, think the same as everyone else.) If she could keep everyone else happy, then, perhaps, would she be happy too?

Years passed, and she gradually lost hope. She learned to dress, talk, and think as the others did. Her world was measured in details, day-timers, and looming deadlines. But on a rare night when she stood small before a canopy of stars, her soul would yearn, just a little. Was life only this, and nothing more? Deep within, she felt the absence of something deep and beautiful. Her soul was hungry for love, but she never truly found it.

Far away, the man had been deeply saddened by her rejection. He would still think of her sometimes. If only she had said yes! He dreamed impossible dreams of what could have been. But he never gave up hope that, someday, she would return to him.

Who could show such love? Can any mortal man love so faithfully? In spite of her rejection, pride, and self-reliance, he still loved her! Would you still love someone who had spurned the best you have? Only one man in all of history could love with such faithfulness and unselfish devotion. Only one would give the ultimate gift to win his beloved.

Jesus Christ is the One Who offers such immense and pure love. He looked on you and loved you as you grew in your mother's womb (Psalm 139:16). He chose the day you would be born, the gifts you would be given, and the family you would enter. He also gave you the priceless gift of your conscience.

Do you remember being a small child and choosing to go against your parents' wishes? Through your conscience, He showed you that it was wrong. Yet, because we are all born with a rebellious nature, you did it anyway. As you grew, you chose to either follow or suppress the voice of your conscience. Either way, your sin has a high price. "For the wages of sin is death…" (Romans 6:23) Every man, woman, and child has earned the penalty of death and eternal punishment for their sins. No amount of good works can "balance" out the weight of our sins. Living a good life cannot wash away our guilt and give us entrance into heaven. God is just, and he cannot allow sin to pass unpunished forever.

Justice demanded that a price be paid, but love stepped in. God the Father sent His only Son, Jesus. Thousands of years ago, He entered earth as a helpless baby. He came to seek and to save the lost (Luke 19:10), and that means you and me! For you, He poured out His lifeblood on the cross. He paid the death penalty for your sins. Jesus offers you forgiveness, freedom, and eternal life with Him. If you will turn from your sins and place your trust in Him, you can be forgiven. He will cleanse you of all your sins and clothe you in white robes of His righteousness.

He passionately pursues you. Jesus penned a Book of precious love letters for you, the Bible. Will you cherish them and delight in reading them? Jesus longs for you to draw near to Him. Have you heard His voice, calling you into His presence? "Come away," He whispers, "and sit at My feet. Come and be Mary for a while." (see Luke 10:42) Will you answer His call?

Too often, both men and women refuse His call, choosing instead to be independent and self-reliant. "I don't have time for that," we think, "Later, I'll seek Him out." We neglect to feed our hungry souls. Our souls were designed for fellowship with Him. God did not create us to be independent robots, never needing rest or renewal. Inherent in our very nature is a need for relationship, for empathy, and for love. God does not leave us alone to stumble through the darkness. He takes the initiative and seeks us out.

God's pursuit of mankind began in the garden of Eden. There, God sought Adam and Eve to walk and talk with them. Genesis 3:8 tells us that, "…they heard the voice of the Lord God walking in the garden in the cool of the day." Adam and Eve knew the voice of God. They had walked and talked with Him many times, tasting the sweetness of His presence. God nourished their souls with His love. In Him, they found satisfaction, joy, and peace. God sought Adam and Eve, and they responded to His love.

Centuries passed, and the time was ripe for God to call out a people for Himself. He chose to call Abram, a wealthy Syrian. Genesis 12:1-3 tells us,

> Now the Lord had said unto Abram, Get thee out of thy country, and from thy kindred, and from thy father's house, unto a land that I will shew thee: And I will make of thee a great nation, and I will bless thee, and make thy name great; and thou shalt be a blessing: And I will bless them that bless thee, and curse him that curseth thee: and in thee shall all families of the earth be blessed.

The Bible does not tell us that Abraham took the initiative to seek God. Rather, God sought Abraham to be the founder of His people. By faith, Abraham believed God and responded in obedience. Throughout Abraham's life, God appeared to him many times. He spoke to Abraham, giving him commands and many priceless promises. As he grew spiritually, Abraham learned to seek the Lord. He responded to God's call and became the first patriarch of the Jewish nation.

Let's fast-forward a generation to the life of Jacob, Abraham's grandson (Genesis 25-36). The second twin of a firstborn pair, Jacob was a greedy, deceptive man. He tricked his older brother Esau into giving up his birthright. Then Jacob deceived his blind father Isaac to steal Esau's blessing. Fleeing Esau's wrath, Jacob journeyed back to Syria to find a wife. He did not seek God's help or guidance, relying instead on his own wits and strength.

One starry night, he arranged stones for his pillows and lay down to sleep. Little did he know that his life was about to change forever.

> And he dreamed, and behold a ladder set up on the earth, and the top of it reached to heaven: and behold the angels of God ascending and descending on it. And, behold, the Lord stood above it, and said, I am the Lord God of Abraham thy father, and the God of Isaac: the land whereon thou liest, to thee will I give it, and to thy seed; And thy seed shall be as the dust of the earth, and thou shalt spread abroad to the west, and to the east, and to the north, and to the south: and in thee and in thy seed shall all the families of the earth be blessed. And, behold, I am with thee, and will keep thee in all places whither thou goest, and will bring thee again into this land; for I will not leave thee, until I have done that which I have spoken to thee of. (Genesis 28:11-15)

Frightened, Jacob awoke, saying, "Surely the Lord is in this place; and I knew it not." He was awed at God's presence and overwhelmed with God's promises. Early the next day, he rose and set up his pillow-stone for a pillar. Solemnly, Jacob made a vow to God.

> If God will be with me, and will keep me in this way that I go, and will give me bread to eat, and raiment to put on, So that I come again to my father's house in peace; then shall the Lord be my God: And this stone, which I have set for a pillar, shall be God's house: and of all that thou shalt give me I will surely give the tenth unto thee. (Genesis 28:20-22)

This was a critical decision in the life of Jacob. Once rebellious, now he promised to serve the Lord. Once proud, now he sought the help of God. God reached down to this struggling man fleeing for his life and set him on a new road. God sought Jacob, and he responded by yielding control of his life. With the blessing of God on his life, Jacob prospered greatly and fathered twelve sons, who became the twelve tribes of Israel.

Long ago, God sought Abraham and Jacob to father and lead His people. Throughout the pages of Scripture, He called individuals to fulfill specific roles in His master plan. God called a desert shepherd named Moses to lead the Hebrew nation out of Egyptian slavery. He selected a young shepherd boy named David to be the first king of Israel. During the Babylonian captivity, God placed a humble girl named Esther in the palace of the king. Through her courage, the Hebrew people escaped certain destruction at the hands of a powerful enemy. God called Isaiah, Jeremiah, and many other prophets to warn His people and foretell the future. In His wisdom, God chose, prepared, and called key people to carry out His plans.

In the New Testament, Christ came and turned the world upside down. God's relationship to man was now shaped by a radically different pattern.

Hebrews 2:9 declares, "But we see Jesus, who was made a little lower than the angels for the suffering of death, crowned with glory and honour; that he by the grace of God should taste death for every man."

Jesus paid the ultimate price to atone for the sins of all people. He came to seek the lost—every man, woman, and child—and call them into His Church. Anyone who freely turns to Christ in faith and repentance can be born again. Each person who turns to Christ is given a specific calling of God on his life. He is spiritually born into the family of God and receives great blessings. Even better, he gains access into the very presence of the Lord Himself.

Today, Jesus is calling all to repentance. The call rings out in Isaiah 55:6-7:

> Seek ye the Lord while he may be found, call ye upon him while he is near: Let the wicked forsake his way, and the unrighteous man his thoughts: and let him return unto the Lord, and he will have mercy upon him; and to our God, for he will abundantly pardon.

Will you seek the Lord today? He offers forgiveness and pardon to you. No matter how dark your past or how far your path has led, He died for your sins. You need only turn to Him, forsake your sin, and ask His forgiveness. He longs to forgive and wash away your sins and give you a new heart. He is seeking you…will you respond to His love?

The story is told of a husband and wife whose marriage was gradually eaten away by unresolved conflict and gnawing discontent. Giving up hope, the wife crossed the ocean in search of a new life. Heartbroken, he wrote letter after letter, begging her to return. He freely admitted his mistakes and begged for her forgiveness. Not once did she respond to these missives of love.

At last, he could endure her silence no longer. He took the next ship and sought her out. Face to face, he humbly sought her forgiveness and asked her to return with him. He was overjoyed and amazed when she accepted readily. He asked, "What made you willing to come home with me? You never responded to all my letters. What changed your mind?" She responded, "This time, you didn't just send me a letter. You came yourself."

Isn't this a precious picture of God's love for us? He wrote letter after letter. He spoke through prophets, kings, and sages. Yet His people mocked, disobeyed, and ignored His words of love. At last, He came Himself. Jesus was born to seek and save the lost. He seeks every man, woman, and child to become His own. Have you responded to the seeking love of God?

As we invite you to seek the Lord with us, this is our prayer for you.

Dear Father,
We thank You for coming to seek and to save us, for giving us Your very best. How deep is Your love, and how limited is our understanding of it! We ask that You would reveal yourself to those who read this book. May they have ears to hear and a heart to seek You with all that they are. For You are our Shield and our exceeding great Reward. May they learn to delight in You, to love You, and to walk with You. We want to see You, Lord. May we never be satisfied with what we know of You. Make us hungry for Your presence, and satisfy us with Your love.
In Christ's lovely Name,
Amen.

CHAPTER 2
Preparing Our Hearts to Seek Him

*"To fall in love with God is the greatest romance;
to seek him the greatest adventure;
to find him, the greatest human achievement."*
-Augustine of Hippo

He was the fourth king of Israel, son of the wisest man on earth. At his father's death, he became heir to a vast kingdom and a formidable military. He had access to the law, the counsel, and the temple of the one true God. His forebears gave him a legacy of priceless testimony, wisdom, and godliness. At the slightest nod of a head, servants would trip over themselves to fulfill his bidding.

His name was Rehoboam. His palace was graced with the finest of Israel's music, art, and culture. His throne was crafted of ivory, overlaid with pure gold, and guarded by twelve carved lions. Politically, his allies were many, his enemies almost non-existent. To a casual observer, his future seemed bright and prosperous.

Fast-forward seventeen years to the end of his reign. What legacy did this king leave for his people? Did he conquer his enemies? Did he lead his people in righteousness? Because he listened to foolish advice, Rehoboam lost ten of his twelve tribes to a rival king. Throughout his reign, he faced the constant headache of war with the ten tribes of Israel.

After establishing his kingdom, he led Israel in forsaking the law of God. In the fifth year of his reign, Shishak king of Egypt marched against Israel. He began by capturing the fenced cities of Judah. Frightened, Rehoboam and his princes humbled themselves. God granted them mercy and promised some deliverance. Reaching Jerusalem, Shishak plundered the rich treasures of temple and palace. He even carried away the shields of gold which Solomon had made. Because of his humility, God's wrath was turned away. Rehoboam narrowly avoided destruction. Despite his godly forebears and powerful position, I think Rehoboam ended his days with many regrets.

Although Rehoboam knew well the difference between good and evil, he chose evil. Why? What motivated the son of the wisest man on earth to live so foolishly? Second Chronicles 12:14 gives us a convicting answer. "And he did evil, because he prepared not his heart to seek the LORD." How can we prepare our heart to seek God? What attitudes should we cultivate in our pursuit of Jesus? In this chapter, we'll focus on three attitudes that are vitally important if we want to see Jesus.

A Repentant Heart

To seek Jesus, we must have a repentant heart. One of Scripture's finest models of repentance is David. The second king of Israel, God called David a man after his own heart. As a teenage shepherd boy, David penned many of the Psalms. He became an assistant to King Saul and behaved himself very wisely. For many years, David patiently waited until the time was ripe for him to become king. At last, David ascended the throne of Israel. Let's zoom our lens in to examine a pivotal episode in David's life.

After eleven years of his reign, the blessing of God is evident. His army has conquered the Philistines, the Moabites, and the Syrians. During this time of blessing and prosperity, David relaxes his guard a little. After all, he no longer has to flee the soldiers of Saul! His country is united behind him. God has given him great victories. Why should he keep going out to battle? Why not just send out his armies? Joab and Abishai are fabulous generals—they can handle the battle! David makes an unwise choice which he will regret for the rest of his life.

While his armies marched out to battle, "David tarried still at Jerusalem." (2 Samuel 11:1) Freed from the strain of responsibility, David is vulnerable to temptation. When he notices a beautiful woman on a rooftop, he yields to desire. Forsaking everything he knows is right, David commits adultery with Bathsheba. A child is conceived, and David panics. He rushes her husband Uriah home from battle to provide a plausible father. But Uriah refuses to go home, not wanting to accept a privilege his fellow soldiers don't have. Desperate, David schemes to have Uriah killed in the front line of battle. His plan succeeds. After mourning for Uriah, Bathsheba becomes the wife of David and bears his son. It would seem that David escaped any consequences.

Is this really the case? Did God really let David get away with adultery, deceit, and premeditated murder? No, God is too holy and just to overlook this sin. The next year, God sent the prophet Nathan to tell David a story.

Nathan recounted a poignant tale of a rich man and a poor man. The rich man had vast flocks and herds of livestock, while the poor man had only one little lamb. He nourished it, shared his own food and cup with it, and loved it deeply. When a traveler visited the rich man, he did not take one of his own sheep. Instead, the rich man cruelly stole the poor man's lamb and killed it for his guest. When David heard this tale, his anger was ignited. He declared, "As the LORD liveth, the man that hath done this thing shall surely die: And he shall restore the lamb fourfold, because he did this thing, and because he had no pity." (2 Samuel 12:5-6)

How did Nathan respond?

Thou art the man.
Thus saith the Lord God of Israel, I anointed thee king over Israel, and I delivered thee out of the hand of Saul;
And I gave thee thy master's house, and thy master's wives into thy bosom, and gave thee the house of Israel and of Judah; and if that had been too little, I would moreover have given unto thee such and such things.
Wherefore hast thou despised the commandment of the Lord, to do evil in his sight? thou hast killed Uriah the Hittite with the sword, and hast taken his wife to be thy wife, and hast slain him with the sword of the children of Ammon.
Now therefore the sword shall never depart from thine house; because thou hast despised me, and hast taken the wife of Uriah the Hittite to be thy wife.
(2 Samuel 12:7-11)

Overcome with conviction, David cries out in repentance. He pours out his heart in Psalm 51, a sincere prayer to God. Seeking God, he finds forgiveness, reconciliation, and peace. In this psalm, let's discover the steps David took on his journey of repentance.

First, David confessed his sin and asked for God's forgiveness. Unconfessed sin bars our entrance into the presence of God. Sin is one of Satan's chief tools for keeping Christians in a state of powerlessness, cut off from the presence of God. It hinders our prayers and breaks our fellowship with other believers. Sin brings guilt, fear, and shame. It robs us of our joy, rest, and confidence. Although confessing your sin can be very difficult, it gives you such freedom! In true confession, we agree with God that we have sinned. We agree that our sin is wrong, against God, and worthy of punishment.

If our story ended at confession, we would, of all men, be most miserable! Yet God has promised to forgive our sins and cleanse us from all unrighteousness (1 John 1:9). He is simply waiting for us to ask Him. Have you neglected to confess a sinful thought, word, or action in your life? Let us pray with the psalmist, "Search me, O God, and know my heart: try me, and know my thoughts: And see if there be any wicked way in me, and lead me in the way everlasting." (Psalm 139:23-24)

After asking for God's forgiveness, David sought restoration to the presence of God. He cried out, "Cast me not away from thy presence; and take not thy holy spirit from me. Restore unto me the joy of thy salvation; and uphold me with thy free spirit." (Psalm 51:11-12) During his period of rebellion, David had not enjoyed sweet fellowship with God. Now he was thirsty and hungry for a taste of God's goodness and the light of His smile. David asked God for joy and restoration into His presence, and God heard his prayers.

Next, David committed himself to obedience. He said, "Then will I teach transgressors thy ways; and sinners shall be converted unto thee." (Psalm 51:13) When we tolerate known sin in our lives, God cannot work through us effectively. If we desire to do great and mighty things, we must confess our sin and choose to obey Him. David demonstrated true repentance. He did not merely turn from sin but also turned to obedience. Obeying God is not difficult to understand, but it is impossible to do in our own strength. Like David, we must seek the power of the Holy Spirit and choose to obey His leading.

As David returned to God, he chose to praise and rejoice. He prayed, "Deliver me from bloodguiltiness, O God, thou God of my salvation: and my tongue shall sing aloud of thy righteousness. O Lord, open thou my lips; and my mouth shall shew forth thy praise." (Psalm 51:14-15) His joy was rekindled at a heavenly flame. Like David, we can rejoice in God's forgiveness, mercy, and restoration. We can get excited about being cleansed and free to serve again! As we inhale the sweet fragrance of freedom, joy begins to bubble up inside our hearts. True joy spills out in sincere praise, thanksgiving, and delight.

Do you rejoice in the forgiveness and restoration of God? If you don't, it is never too late to begin! Ask Jesus to remind you of the depravity of your sin and the depths of His mercy. Learn to rejoice in His forgiveness. It is truly a sweet fountain that will never run dry.

Submission

Sometimes, we seek Jesus half-heartedly. We keep Him at arm's length, afraid that He might ask us to do something we would rather not do. We desire only a comfortable amount of interaction. Perhaps a little pat on the back and, "Keep up the great work!" would be encouraging. But we'd rather not hear Him say, "You know that nosy neighbor next door? Invite her over for dinner. She needs to hear about Me."

The truth is that Jesus pushes us to take risks for Him. He is completely powerful, infinitely wise, and in charge. We're not. He is our Master, and we owe Him unquestioning obedience. Yes, He may ask you to do something hard, or something new, or something that makes no sense to you. Is He your Lord? Doesn't He know everything? Since the answer is yes, we ought to obey Him. When we hear Him speak, we are responsible to obey or face consequences.

In the classic allegorical novel *The Lion, The Witch, and The Wardrobe*, C. S. Lewis demonstrates this truth through dialogue between two of the characters. Susan and Mr. Beaver are discussing Aslan, a lion who typifies Christ. Here are their words.

> "Aslan is a lion- the Lion, the great Lion." "Ooh," said Susan. "I'd thought he was a man. Is he--quite safe? I shall feel rather nervous about meeting a lion." "Safe?" said Mr. Beaver..."Who said anything about safe? 'Course he isn't safe. But he's good. He's the King, I tell you."

We can trust Christ because He is good. Though He is not "safe," Christ is absolutely trustworthy. If we walk by faith even when we can't see the next step, our feet will find the Rock beneath.

Seeking Him also exposes us to His Word. The Word can be uncomfortable, divisive, and unexpected. Convicted by a passage about holiness, you may recognize your need to give up a friendship or a hobby. Reading a passage on giving, you may be challenged to give to a specific need. If you read a passage on words, and your tongue is still intact, oh boy! You will be convicted into the middle of next Friday! Admittedly, keeping Him at arm's length is safer and more comfortable. But, think of what you will miss!

For many people, submitting their future is painful. If you hesitate to give your future to God, ask yourself, "Why am I hesitating?" Too often, we tolerate irrational fears. *"If I surrender, I'll end up a martyr for the faith on a Polynesian island!" "I'll be stuck in a dead-end job forever!" "I'll never get married...or I'll have to marry someone I don't really like!" "God will tell me to _____(fill in the blank)!"* Acknowledge your fears and confess them to God. He won't be surprised since He already knows them. "For God hath not given us the spirit of fear; but of power, and of love, and of a sound mind." (2 Timothy 1:7) After acknowledging your fears, repent of them. Choose to place yourself entirely at God's disposal.

Your loving Father has the best plan for you. From His vantage point outside our space-time reality, He can see every possible scenario for your future. Because He loves you, He will guide your steps in a good path. God has promised not to fail or forsake you (Hebrews 13:5). The One Who spoke the universe into existence has every resource you could possibly require. The psalmist wrote in Psalm 37:25, "I have been young, and now am old; yet have I not seen the righteous forsaken, nor his seed begging bread." Trust God to meet your needs. Give your future to Him.

True submission includes not only your future plans but also your present choices. In your daily walk, are you responsive to the Spirit's direction? When He nudges you to give or serve or pray, do you obey? A submitted heart responds by gladly obeying the direction of God. It is simple to pray, "Lord, I surrender my life to you." It is much harder to flesh out that huge decision in a thousand tiny choices. But it is in the tiny choices that the battle of true submission is won or lost. If you truly desire to know Jesus, you must start here. In the next tiny choice, obey Him.

Submitting to Jesus is far better than clutching the reins of your life. When you submit, you step onto a path better than any you could devise. You discover rest, joy, and peace. Even better, you find yourself in His sweet presence. Submission is indeed the best choice you can make.

From Claudine

One of the turning points of my youth was a simple decision to submit. It was a sweltering July night at Bible camp. The camp director challenged us as campers to ask ourselves, "Is God calling me to full-time Christian ministry?" He told us that God might be calling some of us to be pastors, missionaries, and full-time workers. I felt the Holy Spirit tug at my heart. Beyond a shadow of a doubt, I knew that He was calling me to ministry. But, in my heart, I rebelled against Him. At the tender age of fourteen, I had other plans. Don't laugh, but my dream was to be a Member of Parliament. I had already purchased a five-year membership for the Party I was going to run for, and I had a few lofty goals in mind. A call to ministry threatened to obliterate my cherished plans. I struggled with the choice before me. Should I submit to God's call or chase my dream? That night, the director encouraged us to submit our lives to God's will. According to camp tradition, every camper had an opportunity to throw a branch into

> a campfire. This action symbolized submitting his life. As I waited to hear my cabin called, my heart beat faster. How could I give up my dream for God? Yet I knew I could not live separated from the presence and blessing of God. I chose to yield my future to the hands of God, and I threw my branch onto the fire. Returning to my seat, I knew that I had made the right decision. Once again, I had peace with the Lord, and a flame of excitement was lit in my heart. Since then, God has given me many opportunities for ministry, including serving as a counsellor at camp. I am so glad I decided to give my future to God. Without that decision, I would have missed out on His best. Submitting can be very difficult, but it is so worth it!

A Desire for Jesus

In the Psalms, David demonstrates for us a sincere desire for Jesus. Study the cry of his heart in Psalm 63:1-3 and 5-6.

> O God, thou art my God; early will I seek thee: my soul thirsteth for thee, my flesh longeth for thee in a dry and thirsty land, where no water is; To see thy power and thy glory, so as I have seen thee in the sanctuary. Because thy lovingkindness is better than life, my lips shall praise thee. My soul shall be satisfied as with marrow and fatness; and my mouth shall praise thee with joyful lips: When I remember thee upon my bed, and meditate on thee in the night watches.

David compares his need for God to a desperate thirst in a barren desert. To him, life is empty without the presence of God. David's sincerity is evidenced by his seeking God early. He is willing to wake early to pray, and he meditates on God in the night. His life is a continual walk with God. Although David has experienced the power and presence of God many times, he is not satisfied. He wants more of Jesus!

Without a sincere desire, you will not draw near to Jesus. We are only as close to God as we want to be. If you don't *really* want to get close, Jesus won't push you. "Draw nigh to God, and he will draw nigh to you." (James 4:8a) God has already demonstrated His great love for you. He calls *you* to respond by seeking His face. Psalm 27:8 tells us, "When thou saidst, Seek ye my face; my heart said unto thee, Thy face, Lord, will I seek." Is this the cry of your heart? Do you desire intimacy with Jesus?

What is the worst enemy of a desire for Jesus? Our complacency is the enemy! Too often, Christians decide, "Okay, let's stop right here. I have enough religion to keep me happy. Let's not get carried away!" They apply the brakes to Jesus' work in their lives. Wary of the unknown, they neglect to seek out the presence of Jesus. Don't be one of them. Don't settle for a comfortable level of Christianity. There are heights of joy and depths of peace you have not yet reached! There are precious truths you have not yet unearthed. There are tasks to be done, wars to be fought, and a race to be won! He is calling…will you seek Him?

When a lady is engaged, everyone within a radius of fifty kilometers knows about it. They've seen the photos [yes, darling, he's so handsome!], heard the stories, and admired the [18 karat, solitaire, princess cut] ring. Just as she is deeply in love with her fiancé, we ought to be deeply in love with Jesus. He deserves to be pursued and adored. When you are in love with Jesus, what are the tell-tale signals? Can others recognize your love for Him?

1) When you have a spare moment, you run to His presence. You leap into His arms and tell Him, "I love You! What did I do to deserve such goodness as You give me?" You bask in His presence, soaking up the warmth of His smile. Prayer is as natural as breathing to you, and you revel in hearing His voice.

2) No sacrifice is too much. You willingly pour out your time, money, and abilities in obedience. You invest in ministries, both your own and those of others. If Jesus points out a need to you, you are more than happy to give generously.

3) You enjoy your devotions! Each day, you open the Bible expectantly, eager to discover a new truth or revel in a dear one. The Holy Spirit teaches you little by little, and you listen carefully for His voice. Devotions are not a heavy duty. Instead, they are refreshing and delightful.

4) When you are weary, you don't give up. Love for Jesus motivates you to keep fighting, praying, and trusting. Though the battle rages heavy and the troops around you begin to retreat, you stand your ground. Come hell or high water, you are on the Lord's side.

5) Your life is filled with real joy. Others ask you, "Why are you so happy?" Even when bad days come, you still count your blessings and say, "The Lord is good to me!" You don't have to fake joy. It flows out of your heart in thankfulness and delight. You rejoice in

life, in blessings, in people, and, most of all, in God. When preachers or singers praise the Lord, something inside you resonates with joy. People are attracted by your sincere joy.

6) You love talking about Jesus. At church, Bible studies, and the coffee shop—you take advantage of every opportunity to brag about Him. Perhaps you share how God answered a specific prayer. Or, you explain to a friend that only Jesus has made you truly happy and met the deepest needs of your soul. The Holy Spirit witnesses to others through your mouth.

Examine your life, and ask yourself, "Are any of these true in my life?" Perhaps they are not true right now. If there lies within your heart a cry, "If only I could have that! If only I could love Jesus like that," there is hope. Call out to Jesus, "I want to see You! Show Yourself to me!" If you sincerely seek Jesus, you will find Him.

Preparing Our Hearts

In our journey to seek the Lord, we need to prepare our hearts. Without the right attitudes, we will not see God. The people you interact with only see the person you choose to portray. They watch your face, your words, and your actions. From these, they form an image of who you are. But God alone sees your heart. He knows your deepest thoughts and desires.

It is both comforting and sobering that God knows our human weakness. Although He does not demand perfection, He does expect us to prepare our hearts. Seeking God must begin with a repentant heart. As flesh and blood, we so often fail, and we need God's cleansing forgiveness. When you are convicted of sin, quickly confess it and ask His forgiveness. If you delay repentance, you may easily forget about it. Unconfessed sin can quickly build up a barrier between you and your Saviour. We must also learn to receive and delight in God's forgiveness. A repentant heart is absolutely essential to seeking God.

Next, develop a heart of surrender. Recognize that, "…the Lord he is God: it is he that hath made us, and not we ourselves; we are his people, and the sheep of his pasture." (Psalm 100:3). We owe everything we are and have to the Lord. Simple obedience is the least we can do. Surrender must include both your future plans and your present choices. If we are honest with ourselves, the problem is not that we don't know what God wants us to do. It is simply that we don't want to do it. If your heart is not surrendered, you will not be close to Jesus. He blesses obedience, not disobedience. If you choose surrender, you will discover a peace and joy you've never known…and priceless time in His presence.

To enter His presence, your heart must have a sincere desire for Jesus. Don't get mired in the swamp of complacency and self-preoccupation. Do you delight in earthly pleasures more than in Him? Has your love for Jesus grown cold? If so, ask Him to kindle the flame of your love again. Feed your love for Jesus by thinking about Him, meditating on His Word, and true worship. Later, we'll study these in more detail. Start by choosing to love Him and seek Him. The more you do so, the more your love for Him will flourish.

Do you want to seek God? You alone have the power to prepare your heart. Seeking God begins with a heart that repents, a heart that surrenders, and a heart that longs for Jesus. If you cultivate these attitudes, you will be rewarded. To return to Augustine's words, let us embark on the greatest adventure…seeking God.

Baby Steps:
-Grab a journal. Write down 3 things you are afraid that God will ask you to do if you surrender completely. Choose to surrender these fears to the Lord. Ask Him to give you courage to obey.
-Ask God to remind you of anything He has asked you to do which you have ignored or forgotten about. Make a game plan to get it done.
-If you haven't already learned it, memorize 1 John 1:9. "If we confess our sins, he is faithful and just to forgive us our sins, and to cleanse us from all unrighteousness."
-Carve 20 minutes out of your schedule, and sit down with Psalm 34 and a journal. Record at least 7 truths you learn about God. Have you found these true in your own life? If so, praise God for it!

CHAPTER 3
The Four Circles

The year is 1491 B.C. Under the mighty hand of God, Israel just hit the superhighway out of Egypt. At the Red Sea, she escaped through towering walls of seawater. From the other shore, she witnessed the demise of her former masters. Moses' song of victory still lingers on her lips. After three months of journeying through the desert, Israel arrives in the wilderness of Mount Sinai and pitches her tents. She is ready to hear from God.

In Exodus 19:4-6, God gives Israel a sacred promise.

> Ye have seen what I did unto the Egyptians, and how I bare you on eagles' wings, and brought you unto myself. Now therefore, if ye will obey my voice indeed, and keep my covenant, then ye shall be a peculiar treasure unto me above all people: for all the earth is mine: And ye shall be unto me a kingdom of priests, and an holy nation…

The people respond, "All that the LORD hath spoken we will do." (Exodus 19:8) The Lord promises to appear to Moses in a thick cloud to give him authority and credibility before Israel. He commands Moses, "Go unto the people, and sanctify them to day and to morrow…be ready against the third day: for the third day the LORD will come down in the sight of all the people upon Mount Sinai." (Exodus 19:10-11) The people are separated from God's presence by visible barriers. Touching the sacred mount is forbidden on penalty of death. The children of Israel prepare themselves and count down the hours till the promised day.

On that day, God appears with thunders, lightnings, a thick cloud, and a very loud trumpet. Hearing this, all the people tremble. They nervously approach the mount and stand at its base. God descends on Mount Sinai in fire, smoke, and an earthquake. When the trumpet reaches a crescendo, Moses speaks.

Wonder of wonders…God answers him out of the smoke and fire. The voice that spoke the worlds into existence stoops to speak with Moses. He calls Moses to the top of the mount, to higher ground. But, immediately, He must send Moses down to warn the people not to break through the barriers. He must also charge the priests to sanctify themselves. How disappointed Moses must be...to be so close to God, yet having to return to warn a rebellious people! But his time is coming.

Next, God gives Moses the Ten Commandments and part of the law in chapters 20-23. In Exodus 24, God summons Moses to come up a second time. This time, He also invites others.

> And he said unto Moses, Come up unto the Lord, thou, and Aaron, Nadab, and Abihu, and seventy of the elders of Israel; and worship ye afar off. And Moses alone shall come near the Lord: but they shall not come nigh; neither shall the people go up with him. (Exodus 24:1-2)

Before he ascends the mount again, he gives the people God's law, sacrifices on a new altar, and sanctifies the covenant. After these preparations, he climbs Mount Sinai again. This time, he journeys with Aaron, Nadab, Abihu, and seventy of the elders of Israel. Let's peek into Scripture to catch a glimpse of Heaven's glory.

> And they saw the God of Israel: and there was under his feet as it were a paved work of a sapphire stone, and as it were the body of heaven in his clearness. And upon the nobles of the children of Israel he laid not his hand: also they saw God, and did eat and drink. (Exodus 24:10-11)

What did those elders think, I wonder, gazing on the glory of the Most High? How humbled and amazed they must have been. Out of the many thousands of Israel, they alone saw the Lord in His glory. However, the best was yet to be.

Next, God calls Moses to come closer and receive tables of stone, the law, and the commandments. Moses and his servant Joshua climb higher up the mount of God. The elders must wait until they return. Moses and Joshua are privileged to see a closer vision of God's glory for six days, until, on the seventh day, something changes.

On the seventh day, God calls to Moses out of the midst of the cloud. Moses enters the cloud and climbs higher into the very presence of God. He spends forty days and forty nights with God. During that time, God gives him seven chapters of the law and commandments for God's people. When He has finished communing with Moses, God gives him "two tables of testimony, tables of stone, written with the finger of God." (Exodus 31:18) What a priceless treasure Moses carried as he descended the mount!

From this account, we learn an essential lesson about seeking God. There are four circles of relationship to God. Here, we recognize the classification of 1) the people, 2) the seventy elders, 3) Moses and Joshua, and 4) Moses alone. Let's examine each of these circles in greater detail. As you read on, ask yourself, "In which circle am I?"

The First Circle: The Many Thousands of Israel

The simple fact of being born Jewish was an immense privilege. Israel alone among all nations of the earth had been singled out for Him. Centuries before, God had given unparalleled promises to Israel. To their founder Abraham, God promised guidance, blessing, and a powerful legacy to all families of the earth. He promised to multiply Abraham's descendants into a nation so vast it could be compared to the dust of the earth.

Before Abraham and Sarah were even expecting a son, he promised to give their children the land of Canaan. God said to Abraham, "Fear not, Abram: I am thy shield, and thy exceeding great reward." What a powerful promise! God would both protect Abraham from evil and reward Abraham with the joy of knowing Him. The Lord even forewarned Abraham of Israel's affliction in Egypt and His mighty deliverance. God formed an everlasting covenant with Abraham's descendants and promised to be their God. God established His relationship with Israel through their founder Abraham.

Can any other people lay claim to such a heritage? None other has received the special blessing, care, and protection that Israel enjoyed. Later, God led the tribes of Israel into Egypt to preserve them during a famine. Years passed, and another pharaoh arose who did not know the Hebrews' God. Fearing a rebellion, he enslaved them in cruel bondage. Israel spent four hundred years in slavery, crying out to the Lord for deliverance. God heard their desperate pleas and sent Moses to lead His people out of Egypt. With a mighty hand, God delivered Israel from bondage. Shortly after this, we arrive at Exodus 24.

Let's take a closer look at the Hebrew people's character. In Exodus 19:4-6, God spoke to them through Moses.

> Ye have seen what I did unto the Egyptians, and how I bare you on eagles' wings, and brought you unto myself. Now therefore, if ye will obey my voice indeed, and keep my covenant, then ye shall be a

> peculiar treasure unto me above all people: for all the earth is mine: And ye shall be unto me a kingdom of priests, and an holy nation...

The people responded, "All that the LORD hath spoken we will do." (Exodus 19:8) Of their own free will, Israel committed to total obedience and submission. Did they live up to this commitment? Unfortunately, the people often failed to obey God. Doubting the providence and provision of God, they complained of their hunger and thirst. Doubting Moses' leadership, they rebelled and sought to replace him with counterfeit leaders.

When the Lord appeared on Mount Sinai, their encounter with Him is very significant. As we stated earlier, the people prepared themselves with washing, abstinence, and sanctification. On the third day, God appeared in glory and great power. Standing at the mountain's base, they witnessed the fire of the Lord and a great earthquake. Why did God reveal Himself to the people in this fearful way?

God's people did not fear Him as they should have. They were presumptuous, self-willed, and rebellious. God showed them His power so that they would fear Him, obey His laws, and follow His servant Moses. The many thousands of Israel only saw God's glory as a fearful, unapproachable Presence.

The people's sin barred them from access into God's presence. They could only stand afar off and wonder at His power. As believers today, sin breaks our fellowship with God. Don't allow the clinging tentacles of sin to choke your spiritual life and hide God's face from your sight.

The Second Circle: Seventy Elders

Ministry is no easy task. It is not for the faint of heart, the easily offended, or the self-centered person. Successful ministries are not built on spacious offices, free-flowing espressos, and elegant letterhead. They are built on blood, sweat, and tears (to borrow the memorable expression of Sir Winston Churchill.) Ministries are built with sleepless nights of prayer, midnight calls to the hospital, and tears with those who mourn. They are built in struggling churches, hole-in-the-wall offices, and inner city ghettos. Authentic ministries do not flourish overnight. They require great courage and perseverance in the face of apparently insurmountable odds. John A. Holt described the demands of ministry well:

> Ministry is giving when you feel like keeping, praying for others when you need to be prayed for, feeding others when your own soul is hungry, living truth before people even when you can't see

results, hurting with other people even when your own hurt can't be spoken, keeping your word even when it is not convenient, it is being faithful when your flesh wants to run away.

As the God-ordained leader of the Hebrew people, Moses knew well this truth. After one particularly trying episode (the people were actually weeping over food selection!), Moses cried out to God in great discouragement. His words echo down through the ages with the heavy burden of ministry and the weariness of his flesh.

> Wherefore hast thou afflicted thy servant? and wherefore have I not found favour in thy sight, that thou layest the burden of all this people upon me? Have I conceived all this people? have I begotten them, that thou shouldest say unto me, Carry them in thy bosom, as a nursing father beareth the sucking child, unto the land which thou swarest unto their fathers? I am not able to bear all this people alone, because it is too heavy for me. And if thou deal thus with me, kill me, I pray thee, out of hand, if I have found favour in thy sight; and let me not see my wretchedness. (Numbers 11:11-15)

These are heavy words indeed. Crying out for help, Moses despaired even to death. But God had a better plan. He commanded Moses to choose seventy men of the elders of Israel. God promised, "And I will come down and talk with thee there: and I will take of the spirit which is upon thee, and will put it upon them; and they shall bear the burden of the people with thee, that thou bear it not thyself alone." Obediently, Moses brought seventy elders to the tabernacle. God took some of the burden and spirit of ministry from Moses and gave it to the seventy elders. When God's Spirit rested on them, they prophesied constantly.

In obedience to God, Moses selected these men to bear great responsibility. Under his leadership, they judged the people of Israel. They possessed authority to execute justice, extending from temporary punishment to the death penalty. When Israel assembled, they held positions of respect and high authority. The elders were responsible to God for their people's actions. They bore the weight of educating the people in God's laws and commands. These elders had a significant ministry. Each one sacrificed time, energy, and personal freedom to serve their people.

God rewarded these elders for their faithfulness. From the many thousands of Israel, only these seventy men ascended Mount Sinai with Moses and Joshua. They gazed on God's glory and saw His splendor. "And they saw the God of Israel: and there was under his feet as it were a paved work of a sapphire stone, and as it were the body of heaven in his clearness."

(Exodus 24:10) Despite their fragile human flesh, they saw the glory of God and lived. God had mercy on them by revealing His glory to them.

Even better, they ate and drank in God's presence. Since ancient times, eating and drinking have signified fellowship and trust. We do not prepare banquets for our enemies or feasts for our foes. Rather, we prepare food for those we love, those we trust, and those with whom we desire fellowship. Doesn't God do the same? God loved these elders. He had lovingly watched them sacrifice and serve. Now He wanted to reward their faithfulness and encourage their hearts. He offered a deeper fellowship to these elders. But even they did not see God in all His glory.

The Third Circle: Joshua and Moses

As the circles become smaller and smaller, the revelation of the glory of God grows brighter. The third circle held only Moses, the leader of all Israel, and a young man named Joshua. Who was Joshua? Why did God choose him for special revelation?

We are first introduced to Joshua in Exodus 17. The Israelites have been doubting God and complaining about their lack of water. Although God provides water from a rock, He is displeased with their lack of faith. Trouble strikes when the Amalekites attack Israel.

Recognizing that he needs to plead for God's intervention, Moses chooses a replacement to command the army. He instructs Joshua, "Choose us out men, and go out, fight with Amalek: to morrow I will stand on the top of the hill with the rod of God in mine hand." (Exodus 17:9) Joshua obeys and fights with Amalek. Backed by Moses' prayers(who was backed by Aaron and Hur's arms), Joshua is rewarded with a decisive victory. After the battle, God says something which seems a little strange. He commands Moses, "Write this for a memorial in a book, and rehearse it in the ears of Joshua: for I will utterly put out the remembrance of Amalek from under heaven."

Why would God specifically command Moses to remind Joshua of this? When would Joshua ever face the Amalekites again? Wasn't he just an ordinary fellow, one of the many thousands of Israel? No, he was not. God had already planned that he would succeed Moses as the next leader of Israel. As leader, Joshua would need to wage war against Amalek. Though Joshua was still a young man, God was grooming him for a greater task.

What set Joshua apart from the thousands of Israel? Scripture records a key insight into Joshua's character in Exodus 33. In this passage, Israel has rebelled against God yet again by committing idolatry and immorality.

God rebuked them and commanded them to take off their ornaments and wait for His judgment. Those who sought the Lord went outside the camp to the tabernacle. When Moses entered the tabernacle, God met and talked with him. At this point, the Bible speaks of Joshua.

> And the Lord spake unto Moses face to face, as a man speaketh unto his friend. And he turned again into the camp: but his servant Joshua, the son of Nun, a young man, departed not out of the tabernacle. (Exodus 33:11)

Why did Joshua stay in the tabernacle? He wanted to see God. Joshua didn't want to miss a single chance to see His glory! He didn't care how long he had to wait or what he had to sacrifice. He was serious about seeking the Lord. Others came and went; Joshua did not leave the tabernacle. What a heart for God!

Notice also that the Bible calls Joshua "his servant." Before he ever commanded the nation of Israel, Joshua was only Moses' servant. He was willing to serve humbly without recognition or applause. Most likely, he had to wash Moses' dusty feet after the long days of travel. Perhaps he carried messages for Moses, jogging through the hot desert sun. His duties were small, tiring, and seemingly unimportant. Yet he faithfully performed them day after day, week after week, and year after year. Why did Joshua choose to be Moses' servant? I believe that he wanted to see God. Since Moses had such a close relationship with God, it made sense that Joshua wanted be his servant. Joshua wanted to learn all he could from Moses about seeking the Lord. He longed to know God for himself.

As Joshua matured, his life bore the fruit of seeking God. One of the twelve men sent to investigate Canaan, he believed that God could lead them to victory. Only he and Caleb trusted God. The other ten men said that victory was impossible. Despite the pressure of their peers' unbelief, Joshua and Caleb challenged their people to boldly enter the Promised Land. When the people refused to listen, God judged both them and the other ten men. Those ten men died by the plague before God. Joshua and Caleb alone were spared because of their faith. God also sentenced Israel to forty years of wandering in the wilderness. Every man that complained would perish in the wilderness, never to set foot in the Promised Land.

In Numbers 27, Moses asked God to select the next leader of Israel. God replies, "Take thee Joshua the son of Nun, a man in whom is the spirit, and lay thine hand upon him; And set him before Eleazar the priest, and before all the congregation; and give him a charge in their sight." (Numbers 27:18-19) After Moses' death, God handed the reins of power to Joshua. He gave Joshua wise counsel, the book of the law, and the promise of His continual presence. Under Joshua's command, Israel entered her Promised Land.

He led the first wave of conquest against her enemies. In battle after battle, Joshua won the victory by God's strength.

What qualified Joshua for special intimacy with God? Numbers 27:18 gives us the answer. God paid Joshua a high compliment by calling him "a man in whom is the spirit." Joshua had the right spirit or attitude...one of humility, submission, and willingness to pay any price to seek the Lord.

The Fourth Circle: Moses Alone

The lens of our thought focuses now on the deepest circle of intimacy. There is simply one man alone with God. Singled out from the multitudes of humanity, Moses alone enters the fourth circle. What gave Moses privileged access to the throne of grace? What set him apart from his people?

Decades before, God singled Moses out for a particular mission. Protected from his very infancy, God placed him in the royal court of Egypt. He grew to manhood as the adopted son of the princess royal. Moses studied under the best scholars, statesmen, and warriors Egypt could offer. God prepared him in the lecture-halls and courts of Egypt. His was a life of luxury, vast power, and privilege. Though he was a prince of Egypt, yet he remembered and feared the God of his fathers. One day, he impulsively killed an Egyptian who was abusing a Hebrew slave. Fearing Pharaoh's wrath, he fled to Midian.

Living in the wilderness, Moses met the priest of Midian. He soon married one of his daughters. Moses worked for his father-in-law, tending livestock. What a career change—from a prince of Egypt to a desert shepherd! During this season of quiet labour, God prepared Moses for a position more powerful than any he had known before. Moses had to learn patience, trust, and utter dependence on God. A deep relationship with God would be absolutely essential to leading His people out of Egypt.

For forty years, Moses served God in the desert as a humble shepherd. He developed one of his most important virtues—that of meekness. Numbers 12:3 states, "(Now the man Moses was very meek, above all the men which were upon the face of the earth.)" Coming from the mouth of God Himself, what high praise this is! Living in the desert, Moses encountered the daily reality of his own need, God's power, and God's all-sufficient grace.

While Moses lived in the desert, the people of God suffered under cruel slavery in Egypt. They cried out to God, and He heard their desperate pleas.

One day, Moses came to the mountain of God with his flocks and herds. The angel of the Lord appeared to Moses in a burning bush. Intrigued, Moses approached it for a closer look. God called to him out of the bush and commanded him to take off his shoes. For Moses now stood on holy ground. What if you and I stood there with Moses? What words would we, trembling, hear from the flaming bush?

> Moreover he said, I am the God of thy father, the God of Abraham, the God of Isaac, and the God of Jacob. And Moses hid his face; for he was afraid to look upon God. And the Lord said, I have surely seen the affliction of my people which are in Egypt, and have heard their cry by reason of their taskmasters; for I know their sorrows; And I am come down to deliver them out of the hand of the Egyptians, and to bring them up out of that land unto a good land and a large…Now therefore, behold, the cry of the children of Israel is come unto me: and I have also seen the oppression wherewith the Egyptians oppress them. Come now therefore, and I will send thee unto Pharaoh, that thou mayest bring forth my people the children of Israel out of Egypt. (Exodus 3:6-10)

Filled with fear and doubts, Moses questioned God. *Are you sure I'm the right man for the job? But what if they ask me your name? What if they don't believe me? Don't You remember that I'm terrible at public speaking?* God answers Moses' questions and gives him clear direction. He even reveals to Moses His great Name, "I AM THAT I AM.". Empowered with all the strength of Jehovah, Moses obeys, returning to Egypt with his family. God punishes the idolatry of Egypt, liberates His people from slavery, and leads them out with power.

Despite Moses' faithful life, he was not a sinless man. At times, he was hasty, hot-tempered, and even rebellious. However, when he sinned, he was humble enough to repent. Moses learned from his mistakes. His heart was humble before the Lord. Moses was a man God could use.

In Exodus 24, he ascended higher than any other man on the mountain of God. We read in wonder, "And the glory of the Lord abode upon mount Sinai, and the cloud covered it six days: and the seventh day he called unto Moses out of the midst of the cloud. And Moses went into the midst of the cloud, and gat him up into the mount: and Moses was in the mount forty days and forty nights." (Exodus 24:16,18) Moses alone entered the cloud of God's glorious presence. During those forty days and nights, he tasted no bread or water. The presence of God alone sustained him.

In Exodus 33, the curtain is drawn aside, and we catch a glimpse of the sweet fellowship Moses tasted. Alone with his creator, he sought to know God. In verse 13, Moses asked, "…show me now thy way, that I may know thee, that I may find grace in thy sight..." God responded, "My presence shall go with thee, and I will give thee rest." (Exodus 33:14) He told Moses, "...thou hast found grace in my sight, and I know thee by name. Then Moses asked, "I beseech thee, shew my thy glory."

Because of Moses' frail humanity, it would be impossible for him to see God's face and live. Instead, God placed Moses in a safe hollow of the rock. When He passed by, God covered Moses with His hand to protect him. Then He took away His hand, allowing Moses to gaze on the glory of God from behind.

> And the Lord passed by before him, and proclaimed, The Lord, The Lord God, merciful and gracious, longsuffering, and abundant in goodness and truth, Keeping mercy for thousands, forgiving iniquity and transgression and sin, and that will by no means clear the guilty; visiting the iniquity of the fathers upon the children, and upon the children's children, unto the third and to the fourth generation. (Exodus 34:6-7)

Overcome with awe, Moses bowed his head to the earth and worshipped. He pleaded, "...go among us; for it is a stiffnecked people; and pardon our iniquity and our sin, and take us for thine inheritance." (Exodus 34:9) God made a covenant with Moses and the children of Israel there.

On that mountain, God also revealed His blueprints for a tabernacle. At last, God would have a place to meet with His people. After giving Moses extensive instructions on building the tabernacle, God says, "And I will dwell among the children of Israel, and will be their God." (Exodus 29:45) What an amazing privilege! Despite Israel's rebellion, complaining, and lack of faith, God would dwell with them. The tabernacle pointed to the future…to the age of grace, when God would dwell within us (Romans 12:1-2).

When Moses came down from Mount Sinai, he did not realize that some of God's glory had rubbed off on him! His skin shone with an unearthly radiance. It was so bright that the people were afraid to approach him. Moses had to wear a veil when he spoke with his people. "But when Moses went in before the Lord to speak with him, he took the vail off, until he came out…" (Exodus 34:34) Moses was so close to God on the mountain that his face shone with his Father's glory! When we seek the Lord, others will notice a difference in us. We will reflect the radiant glory of God when we truly seek Him with all our heart.

Like Moses, we can know the joy of God's presence. We should cultivate an attitude of meekness. Like Moses, we should submit to God's will even when we do not understand. Let's follow Him even when He leads us through a barren wilderness. Let's seek His face early. For He is a rewarder of those who diligently seek Him!

In Which Circle Are You?

Are you one of the people, only seeing God afar off? For the vast majority of Israel, sin separated them from the glory of God. They knew Him only as a distant, unapproachable King, not a precious Father. Maybe you have wandered from the presence of God because of personal sin. If God seems far away, who moved?

Are you one of the seventy elders? Like them, you may serve God faithfully. But something still lacks. Perhaps, like Martha, you are busy with many things and neglect to sit at Jesus' feet.

Are you in the third circle with Moses and Joshua? Perhaps you have gone beyond merely outward service to serving with all your heart. Like Joshua, you seek both the presence and the active work of God in your life. No sacrifice is too great, and no obstacle too big for your quest. You know enough of Jesus to long for more.

Are you in the fourth circle with Moses alone? Like him, you walk humbly with the Lord. Recognizing your own frailty, you lean on His strength. You have been unusually blessed with the presence and hand of God on your life. People see the light and love of Jesus shining through your life.

No matter what circle you are in today, know that Jesus wants you to seek Him. He calls you to greater fellowship in James 4:8a, "Draw nigh to God, and he will draw nigh to you..." Like the elders, be faithful in serving God. Like Joshua, purpose to seek Jesus no matter what the cost. Like Moses, humble yourself before Him. If you seek Jesus with all your heart, you too can gain access into the deepest circle of His presence.

CHAPTER 4

Seeking Him in Prayer

Isaiah 65:24
And it shall come to pass, that before they call, I will answer; and while they are yet speaking, I will hear.

Seeking God must begin in the secret place, in the quiet of our personal time with God. When we make seeking God our first priority, this tells Him, "I love you." When we rise in the morning, our first thought should be of our Saviour. Even if we choose to have the bulk of our devotional time later in the day, we must begin by talking to Jesus. I love a C. S. Lewis quote that describes the necessity of seeking Him first.

> It comes the very moment you wake up each morning. All your wishes and hopes for the day rush at you like wild animals. And the first job each morning consists simply in shoving them all back; in listening to that other voice, taking that other point of view, letting that other larger, stronger, quieter life come flowing in. And so on, all day. Standing back from all your natural fussings and frettings; coming in out of the wind.

When we begin our day with prayer, we align our compass to true north. We acknowledge our dependence on God and ask for His help and presence in our day. Though we have troubles and pressing concerns, we must learn to quiet the clamour of mental must-dos and what-ifs. We must be still and listen for His voice (Psalm 46:10). In this chapter, we'll examine how to seek God in prayer.

Focusing our Minds on Him

As we seek God in prayer, we must focus our minds completely on Him. In Psalm 46:10, God commands us, "Be still, and know that I am God: I will be exalted among the heathen, I will be exalted in the earth." Often, we enter the presence of God with a mind still buzzing with the cares of this world, a heart distracted. We must learn to still our hearts and minds and fix our gaze on Him. How can we do this?

First, let's turn our phones on vibrate and leave them in another room. Nothing can turn us away from God's Spirit faster than a distraction with the things of this world. Texting, the Internet, and social media have great potential to steal your heart away from God. They can breed an intense attachment and even addiction. We are commanded to love nothing more than God. First John 2:15-16 warns us, "Love not the world, neither the things that are in the world. If any man love the world, the love of the Father is not in him. For all that is in the world, the lust of the flesh, and the lust of the eyes, and the pride of life, is not of the Father, but is of the world." Have you been distracted by the world? Have you allowed a love for this world and its things to enter your heart? Beware of losing your first love. Guard your time with God jealously.

Second, Peter shares with us the key to a peaceful mind in 1 Peter 5:6-7. "Humble yourselves therefore under the mighty hand of God, that he may exalt you in due time: Casting all your care upon him; for he careth for you." In prayer, we humble ourselves under God's hand. We acknowledge our constant need for His grace. Prayer demonstrates in a tangible way our dependence on our Master. In prayer, we commit ourselves into His hands. We cast all our worries, fears, and hopes at His feet. We trust that He will tenderly pick them up, sift out the grain, and blow away the chaff. After leaving our cares with Him, we can walk away free. He can handle our problems much better than we can. As we approach His throne, we must first cast all our cares on Him.

Confession

When we seek a holy God, we must have a clean heart. Psalm 66:18 tells us, "If I regard iniquity in my heart, the Lord will not hear me…" Though our sins have been washed away by Christ's blood, we still need restoration to God's fellowship after we have sinned. 1 John 1:9 is a precious verse to the believer, "If we confess our sins, he is faithful and just to forgive us our sins, and to cleanse us from all unrighteousness." Before seeking God, we must acknowledge specific sins that we've committed and ask His forgiveness.

Worship

After being cleansed, we turn our gaze to Him. In Psalm 105:1-4, the psalmist gives us a model of Biblical worship.

> O give thanks unto the Lord; call upon his name: make known his deeds among the people. Sing unto him, sing psalms unto him: talk

ye of all his wondrous works. Glory ye in his holy name: let the heart of them rejoice that seek the Lord. Seek the Lord, and his strength: seek his face evermore.

Worshipping God includes thanksgiving. We can either write down some of the current blessings God has given us or simply thank Him aloud for them. Has God given you good health, grace for today, your daily bread(and ice cream!), and the guidance of His Spirit? Thank Him! Every good gift and every perfect gift comes from His hand (James 1:17). Thanksgiving focuses our minds on God's generosity.

According to Psalm 105:2, worship includes singing praises to God. Music is a powerful tool we can employ in worship. One godly man who understood true worship would simply use an old hymnbook and his Bible. He would choose a hymn, sing through a line or two, and put it into his own words. For example, he might sing, "And can it be that I should gain An int'rest in the Savior's blood? Died He for me, who caused His pain?" [Charles Wesley] Then he would cry out, "Saviour, what great love You have for me! I will never be worthy of such grace. Thank You for that precious blood! Thank You for the pain and suffering You endured for me." He would continue through a whole hymn in the same manner.

In your time of worship, try using a hymnbook. Or sing along with a CD of music focused on worshipping God. When you use music, be careful to keep your focus on Jesus. Don't be distracted by thinking about how your voice sounds or the quality of the music. Also, beware of using external music too often. You need to hear Jesus' still, small voice in a quiet place. If you get a great song stuck in your mind, you may not be able to hear anything else well! Just be aware of the potential of music to be a distraction. However, God created music to worship Him. When we sing heartfelt praise to Him, it is a sweet sound in His ears.

Next, the psalmist exhorts us to "talk ye of all his wondrous works." (Psalm 105:2) Has God saved you? Is there evidence of His loving hand in your life? When you gaze through the mist of years past, do you see the guidance of a faithful God? Then let the redeemed of the Lord say so! (Psalm 107:2) Remind yourself of God's wondrous works in your life—His salvation, guidance, provision, protection—and in the lives of others.

The Bible is rich with the stories of lives God has touched. Praise God for leading Moses and the children of Israel through the wilderness. Thank Him for using Esther to save her people. Praise Him for opening salvation to the Gentiles. Thank Him for healing the widow's son. When you rehearse God's mighty works, you encourage your own heart and strengthen your faith.

According to verse 3, we should glory in His holy Name. We can find much material for worship in the names of God. The Bible gives us many names of God. Each name reveals a different facet of His character and His ways. God is Jehovah, which means, "I Am That I Am." This Name shows that He is eternal and unchanging, One we can rely upon. God the Son is the Prince of Peace. In Him we discover true peace that the world cannot offer. God the Son is also our great High Priest. He alone offered the final sacrifice, washing us from our sins in His precious blood. These are but a few of the Names of God we can employ in our worship. Search for more, and you will discover rich truths about our God.

As we worship, what should be our attitude? The psalmist answers this question in Psalm 103:3b, "…let the heart of them rejoice that seek the Lord." The true worshipper feasts his eyes on the reality of God and delights in Him. Learning to delight in God is the foundation of true joy. If we base our happiness on people, we will be disappointed. If we base our joy on personal success, we will be discouraged by failure. But happiness based on Jesus will never fail. He is the Well of living waters that will never run dry! Learn to say, "I am happy simply because Jesus loves me, and I am His. How good He is to me!" When we truly worship, we will find joy in Him.

Sometimes, we may be perplexed and discouraged. In these times, we must resolve with the psalmist, "My heart is fixed, O God, my heart is fixed: I will sing and give praise." (Psalm 57:7) God is always worthy of worship, for He never changes. By worshipping Him, our seemingly insurmountable trials will shrink down to manageable size. We will find comfort in His promises and rest in His peace. Even in difficult times, we should firmly resolve, "I will worship Him, for He is worthy."

Requests

God delights in hearing the prayers of His people…and that means you! Not only that, but He wants you to ask for things. In John 16:24, Jesus told the disciples, "Hitherto have ye asked nothing in my name: ask, and ye shall receive, that your joy may be full." When we ask for things in line with His will, God delights in saying, "Yes!" What do you truly want? What is the secret longing of your heart? If it lines up with His will as revealed in the Bible, ask boldly! Write down your request and the date you began to ask for it. Pray for it faithfully. Wait patiently, in expectation for His answer. Do be careful what you pray for. He answers prayer!

The Posture of Prayer

The posture we choose can help us pray with a reverent attitude. When he dedicated the temple, Solomon offered a lengthy prayer before all Israel.

"And it was so, that when Solomon had made an end of praying…he arose from before the altar of the Lord, from kneeling on his knees with his hands spread up to heaven." (1 Kings 8:54) The posture of kneeling brings us lower, reminding us that we are only sinners saved by grace. Kneeling in prayer can be a helpful habit. When we are on our knees, our minds can focus on God more easily. We are freed from the distractions of constant activity and reminded of our need for God. Kneeling is an excellent posture for prayer (assuming you are physically able).

In 2 Samuel 7, we discover another posture of prayer. Out of his heart for God, David has just offered to build a temple. But God tells him that, because of his wars, he is not qualified to build a temple of peace. Yet God encourages David by promising to bless his son and establish his kingdom forever. Overcome with God's goodness, David enters the temple to pray. "Then went king David in, and sat before the Lord, and he said, Who am I, O Lord God? and what is my house, that thou hast brought me hitherto?" (2 Samuel 7:18) Since the tabernacle did not have chairs or benches, I think it's safe to assume David sat upon the floor. Seated in the dust, he showed humility and thankfulness. Before his eyes stretched out the glories of gold and tapestry, blue and scarlet. To think that the Designer of all this would bless him and his family with such kindness! David was humbled and worshipped God for His great goodness. We too can sit before the Lord and worship.

In Genesis 17:3, Abraham fell on his face, and God talked with him. Sometimes, we too can prostrate ourselves on the ground before God. When we lie face-down before God, we are vulnerable and helpless. This posture symbolizes trust and shows submission to God. In this position, we can close our eyes, take a deep breath, and focus our thoughts on God. We can still our racing thoughts and listen for His voice. (However, if you are physically unable to lie facedown, this does not diminish your prayers, your submission, or God's respect for your prayer.) Lying prostrate before the Lord can be a helpful posture of prayer.

However, God answers sincere prayers even in unusual postures. In Matthew 14, the disciples are travelling across the Sea of Galilee. Fighting weariness, they also wrestle to sail the ship forward through turbulent winds and a stormy sea. In the middle of the night, they are shocked to see a silhouette striding calmly on the sea. Alarmed, they cry out in fear. But it is Jesus! He tells them, "Be of good cheer; it is I; be not afraid." (Matt. 14:27) Bold, impetuous Peter shouts across the waves, "Lord, if it be thou, bid me come unto thee on the water." Jesus says, "Come." And Peter steps out in faith onto the raging waves. After just a few steps, he takes his eyes off Jesus and notices the blustering wind. Suddenly afraid, Peter begins to sink rapidly beneath the waves. In desperation, he cries, "Lord, save me."

Immediately, Jesus reaches out His hand to Peter and rescues him. "O thou of little faith, wherefore didst thou doubt?" He asks. In the stormy Sea of Galilee, Peter had no time to sit or kneel or even lie prostrate. Sinking beneath the waves, he had just enough time to cry to Jesus. But his desperate call for help was enough. Jesus hears the cry of the humble regardless of their situation or posture.

Praying Scripture

In the Bible, God has given us a priceless treasure….the collected prayers of a host of saints of old. Scattered throughout the Old and New are petitions for every circumstance, from pleading for help to shouting for joy. Psalms overflows with raw, candid prayers and praises. We can employ the prayers of the Bible by praying Scripture back to God. I like to take a whole chapter and pray through it, finding gems that I can praise & thank God for. When we pray Scripture, we are using the very words of God. God promises that His Word will accomplish His purpose and not return void (Isaiah 55:11). Praying Scripture is much more powerful than just praying our own words. As a bonus, you will become very familiar with your Bible if you pray Scripture to God daily. Here are some jumping-off points to help you get started.

To Praise Him: Isaiah 12, 25, 49; Psalm 107, 118, 144; Hebrews 8; Revelation 4

For Others: Ephesians 1:15-23 and 3:14-19; Philippians 1:9-11; Colossians 1:9-12; John 17:11-21, 24, 26; John 15:4-14; Isaiah 26:2-4

For Yourself: Psalm 37, 63, 91; Zephaniah 3:14-17, Malachi 3:16-18; Romans 6:11-14; Romans 8:1-6, 13-14; Romans 12; 1 Timothy 4:13-16

Prayer is one of the cornerstones of seeking God. In the quiet of our time with Him, we are free at last to spill out the cares, fears, and heartaches we bear. In Psalm 62:8, He commands us, "Trust in him at all times; ye people, pour out your heart before him: God is a refuge for us. Selah." Nothing you say will take Him by surprise, but He wants to hear it from your lips. When you truly love someone, you enjoy listening to them, even if their words are well-used and time-worn. Seeking God through prayer is the portal to a life of happiness and knowing Him. Will you walk through it?

Baby Steps:
- Write down one action God has told you to do which you have put off. Make a clear game plan to do it this week.
- Choose three specific prayer requests. Record them in your journal or a Notes app on your phone. Commit to pray for them every day.

- Pray Psalm 103 back to God.
- Choose three Names of God. Research their original meanings and their significance to New Testament believers. Record what you learn.

From Claudine

I will never forget a prayer I heard in a small country church one sweltering Sunday morning. I don't even remember what the sermon was about. I couldn't tell you the text or a single one of the points. But I remember how the pastor spoke to God as a very dear Friend. In his closing prayer, he prayed something like this, "Lord, we come to You as a needy people. You know we have many problems. There are heartaches and grief. There are people that are suffering and hurting. But, Lord, we have You...and that is enough." The way he prayed his last sentence touched me deeply. He spoke it with such deep tenderness and love. No matter how great the pain, no matter how deep the loss, he knew that God would carry him through it. I thought, "I don't know God like he does. But I want to!" That afternoon, through bittersweet tears, I humbled myself before God and purposed to seek Him with all my heart. I found joy, peace, and delight in His presence. God used a simple prayer to break through my self-satisfied complacency and draw me to Himself. I will always be grateful for a pastor's simple prayer that inspired me to seek God.

CHAPTER 5
Seeking Him in Bible Study

To get the full flavor of an herb, it must be pressed between the fingers, so it is the same with the Scriptures; the more familiar they become, the more they reveal their hidden treasures and yield their indescribable riches.
– John Chrysostom, A.D. 347-407

God has given us a matchless treasure in His revealed Word. When we seek God in the pages of the Bible, we can see Him through eyes of faith. We can hear His voice, understand His truth, and claim His power. The Word is an ever-deepening river of blessing and life. As we dive deeper into it, we realize more and more the smallness of our knowledge and the greatness of His wisdom. The more we love it, the more we glimpse the glory of God shining from every page. The Bible is both the only reliable *history* of our planet and, far better, it is *His Story*.

Throughout the Bible, God commands us to actively pursue wisdom. Speaking through the pen of Solomon, He calls us to seek wisdom.

> "My son, if thou wilt receive my words, and hide my commandments with thee; So that thou incline thine ear unto wisdom, and apply thine heart to understanding; Yea, if thou criest after knowledge, and liftest up thy voice for understanding; If thou seekest her as silver, and searchest for her as for hid treasures; Then shalt thou understand the fear of the Lord, and find the knowledge of God." (Proverbs 2:1-5)

Notice the progression of the action verbs. We begin by simply receiving His Word. As we recognize its value, we incline our ears to hear wisdom. Hungry to know more, we cry out for knowledge and understanding. We invest time, energy, and possessions to learn more wisdom. Then, (and, oh, what a happy *then!*) we will understand the fear of the Lord and *find the knowledge of God*. If we search for true wisdom, our path will lead straight to the feet of Jesus! "In whom are hid all the treasures of wisdom and knowledge." (Colossians 2:3) If we seek wisdom in His Word, we can know Him! What greater reward can we ask?

To seek God in His Word, we must prepare our hearts. In chapter 1, we talked about how God seeks us for salvation. Have you responded in faith and repentance to His free offer of salvation? As we discussed in chapter 2, your heart needs to be submitted to Him. Are you prepared to obey the truth you will learn in His Word? Are you willing to give up sin in your life? Let's examine our hearts and ask ourselves if we are completely submitted to God. If not, let's yield to Him and be willing to change as He directs us.

Another key requirement to seeking God in His Word is faith. Hebrews 11:6 declares, "But without faith it is impossible to please him: for he that cometh to God must believe that he is, and that he is a rewarder of them that diligently seek him." Faith is defined as "belief and trust in and loyalty to God," according to the Merriam-Webster Dictionary. Faith is a simple choice to believe that the Bible is God's very words given to us. It has been inspired by His Spirit and preserved through millennia. Though we will never fully understand it on this side of Heaven, we choose to trust its authority. We believe that it is free from error and corruption.

Read the words of John Wesley, a great 18th-century English preacher and writer. He made a convincing argument for divine inspiration.

> The Bible must be the invention either of good men or angels, bad men or devils, or of God.
> 1. It could not be the invention of good men or angels; for they neither would nor could make a book, and tell lies all the time they were writing it, saying, 'Thus saith the Lord,' when it was their own invention.
> 2. It could not be the invention of bad men or devils; for they would not make a book which commands all duty, forbids all sin, and condemns their souls to hell for all eternity.
> 3. Therefore, I draw this conclusion, that the Bible must be given by divine inspiration.

It is absolutely essential that we believe the Bible is God's literal, preserved Word. If we do not, what is our authority? On what can we rely? Experience alone is not a sufficient guide to know God.

Perhaps someone may say, "I don't need the Bible. I can experience God through His creation." But creation is only the general revelation of God. It reveals His character and motivates us to seek Him further. But, we cannot learn of Christ or forgiveness or repentance through the stars and sunsets.

Only in the Bible can we learn the concrete truth our souls need. Only in its wisdom can we find a reliable path for our feet. Let's choose to seek God in Scripture with a heart of faith.

Why Study the Bible?

The story is told of an African diplomatic delegation who visited Queen Victoria in the early 19th century. She was the monarch of the British Empire, which held vast sway around the globe. Reaching from Australia to Africa, from Canada to the British Isles, the sun never set on the British Empire of her day. Curious, one diplomat questioned her about the secret to Britain's rise to power.

Victoria made no mention of her mighty armies, her extensive navy, or her prosperous commerce. She did not point to her vast wealth or loyal people. Instead, she handed him a richly bound Bible, saying, "What is the secret of England's superiority among the nations? Go tell your prince that this is the secret of England's political greatness." At that moment in history, England was mighty because its people had loved, studied, and followed the teachings of the Bible.

Why should we study the Bible? Let's examine 9 key reasons for consistent and careful study of God's Word.
1) It cleanses our mind and heart from evil. Ephesians 5:26 speaks of Christ's ministry to the church. "That he might sanctify and cleanse it with the washing of water by the word,"
2) It motivates us to live holy lives. Christ prayed for us, "Sanctify them through thy truth: thy word is truth." (John 17:17)
3) It strengthens our conscience. "Wherewithal shall a young man cleanse his way? by taking heed thereto according to thy word." (Psalm 119:9)
4) It exalts Jesus Christ. Christ said, "Lo, I come: in the volume of the book it is written of me," in Psalm 40:7.
5) It wounds pride by revealing our sin. Isaiah lights a match to man's self-righteousness, and it goes up in a blaze of painful flames. "But we are all as an unclean thing, and all our righteousnesses are as filthy rags; and we all do fade as a leaf; and our iniquities, like the wind, have taken us away." (Isaiah 64:6)
6) It reveals the motives and thoughts of our hearts. Paul tells us in Hebrews 4:12, "For the word of God is quick, and powerful, and sharper than any twoedged sword, piercing even to the dividing asunder of soul and spirit, and of the joints and marrow, and is a discerner of the thoughts and intents of the heart."
7) It equips you to do good works and serve others. "All scripture is given…That the man of God may be perfect, throughly furnished unto all good works." (2 Timothy 3:16-17)

8) It disturbs our routines and comfortable complacency. The psalmist writes, " I thought on my ways, and turned my feet unto thy testimonies." (Psalm 119:59) When confronted with the truth of the Bible, we realize that our ways miss the mark and fall short of God's perfect standard.

9) It demands obedience. Christ Himself gave us the acid test of our love for God in John 14:15. "If ye love me, keep my commandments."

How to Study the Bible

Studying the Bible is absolutely vital in our quest to seek the Lord. Here are some quick tips to make the most of your time in the Word.

- Choose a time of day when your energy levels and mental attention are high. If you are exhausted or (for some of us) pre-caffeine, you will not be able to focus and learn as much as you would otherwise. Give the Lord your best time, not your leftovers.
- Purchase a notebook…and I don't mean one of those tiny, cramped memo pads. Get the sort of notebook you would give to your best friend for her birthday, with widely spaced lines and quality paper. Indigo has an amazing selection of charming notebooks, but you can also snag decent ones at Walmart or even Dollarama. If you get a quality notebook, it will survive daily use, getting dropped in the snowbank on the way to church, and tears when the truth of His goodness hits home. You'll get to read it years later and treasure the truths you've proven true since the time you recorded them.
- Find a quiet, well-lit place to sit with your Bible and notebook.
- We recommend leaving your phone in another room, turned on airplane mode. It can be a huge distraction. If the call is urgent, they'll just leave a message for you.
- It may be a good idea to tell other members of your household, "I've decided to work on being consistent in my devotions. Every day at this time, I'm going to do Bible study. I won't be available during this time. Can I make adjustments in our routine to make sure this works for you, too?"
- Make a commitment to read a regular portion every day. If you are just beginning to study God's Word, you can start with a chapter every day. You have lots of options! Some people enjoy working through Bible study guides that give assigned reading and questions. Others read through the Bible in a year. You can read through the Old and New Testaments simultaneously. Numerous websites and apps offer Bible reading plans and accountability tools. If you start a Bible reading plan and get bored, you can always switch to a different one. The key is to keep reading it!

- For every chapter you read, choose a few of the best verses. Write them out to help you remember them.
- Ask good questions. One helpful tool for studying a passage is the SPECK method.
  Sin: Is there a sin to confess and avoid?
  Promise: Does God give a promise to us?
  Example: Does this passage describe positive and negative examples? What actions and qualities are praised? Which are condemned?
  Command: What does God command me to do? What does He forbid me to do? How can I obey His commands today?
  Knowledge: What do I learn about God the Father, Jesus, and the Holy Spirit? What are His actions, attitudes, and attributes? What does He love? What does He hate?
- Persevere even during seasons when you struggle with studying your Bible and when God seems far away. Remember the struggles and doubts Job faced. Despite his immense trial, Job trusted in the Lord. Isaiah 50:10 encourages us during such times, "Who is among you that feareth the Lord, that obeyeth the voice of his servant, that walketh in darkness, and hath no light? let him trust in the name of the Lord, and stay upon his God." Wait for His light at the end of your tunnel—stay faithful!

7 Key Principles for Bible Study

As we study the Bible, we will encounter statements, facts, and ideas we are unfamiliar with. How can we learn to rightly divide the Word and understand it? To properly understand the Bible, we can use these helpful principles.

1. The Literal Principle

   Much of God's Word should be taken in the strictest literal sense. When it states that God created the heavens and the earth, we believe it. David Cooper said, "When the plain sense of Scripture makes common sense, seek no other sense."
   However, God's Word does contain some figurative language. When Christ said, "I am the bread of life," He did not actually mean that He was literally bread. (John 6:35) In such a case, we should study the passage to determine its symbolic meaning.

2. The Contextual Principle

   Always interpret a verse in the light of the verses immediately before and after it. Entire doctrines and cults have been based on single verses taken completely out of context. Out of context, you can easily misunderstand and misapply verses. Psalm 82:6 states, "I have said, Ye are gods; and all of you are children of the most High." Does this verse teach that men are gods? Certainly not! Psalm 82 speaks of man's frailty and short life in the very next verse. But, stripped from context, it would be easy to misunderstand. Consider how verses are influenced by their surrounding verses.

3. The Historical Principle

Does this verse have a meaning specific to a certain time period or culture? Is this a verse written only for the priests, the disciples, or the Levites? What group is the author addressing? Obviously, we as Gentile believers today don't have to follow the Old Testament ordinances and sacrificial system. We can still learn principles and truths from it, however.

To help you understand this principle better, look at the notes in a Scofield Reference Bible. Bible scholars have divided world history into seven "dispensations." These are specific periods of God's dealing with mankind. Each is governed by different principles and policies. Currently, we are living in the Age of Grace/the Church Age. During this period, salvation is open to both Jews and Gentiles. Christ has ordained that we spread the gospel to the four corners of the earth. The riches of God's grace have been opened to all the world. These truths colour and deepen our understanding of verses written for and during the Age of Grace. Other dispensations have different guiding principles. Always try to understand the historical and cultural context of the passage you are studying.

4. The Grammatical Principle

To understand a verse better, consider its grammar and syntax. What words are used? What are their parts of speech? How do they fit together and influence each other? What punctuation is used? We believe God has preserved every jot and tittle. Don't be afraid to get out a dictionary, thesaurus, or lexicon—or simply find one online. You will glean so much more truth if you study words in more detail. Each one is God-breathed and essential to our comprehension.

5. The Synthetical Principle

If you are still struggling to understand a verse, search an online Bible or concordance to find verses with the same topic or keywords. Pay special attention to the earliest mention of your keyword in Scripture. The principle of first mention tells us that the first mention in Scripture defines it. Consider all the verses you find as a group. Which verses are clear and simple to understand? Interpret your difficult verse in the light of more straightforward verses.

6. The Typical Principle

    Some ideas, people, activities, and items are "types" or symbols God uses repeatedly in Scripture. Oil is a type of the Holy Spirit. The fig tree is a type of Israel. Adam was a type of Christ. When you encounter verses about oil, they may or may not be about the Holy Spirit. But there is a good chance that they will contain symbolic truth. Types can provide material for fascinating study and learning. Ask your pastor for a list of Biblical types (and perhaps even verses) for your personal study. You will be amazed at the rich meaning hidden just below the surface of your Bible reading!

7. The Practical Principle

    In Psalm 119:34, the psalmist prays, "Give me understanding, and I shall keep thy law; yea, I shall observe it with my whole heart." He made a practical connection between understanding the Bible and obeying it. For him, Bible study was not just a pleasant activity or a mental exercise. It shaped the clay of his choices, influenced the game plan of his goals, and set ablaze the flame of his love for God. Will we be doers of the Word, or just hearers? Let's allow the Word to carve us into His likeness, one chip at a time.

A sweet relationship with God, just like any other, is built with a million tiny choices.

Love says, "Since I have a crazy busy day tomorrow, I'll get up early to read my Bible."

Love says, "I have no clue what to do in this situation. What does the Bible say about it?"

Love says, "I can't wait to check the score from last night's game. But I need to read my Bible first."

Love says, "Even though I'm tempted to do what feels good, remember that verse I read the other day? God already gave me a way of escape from this temptation. I'm going to say no and walk away!"

Love says, "I can't see past the next step. But I trust God's goodness. I'm going to step forward in faith."

Sometimes, love has to tell itself, "Stop right there. You're being selfish. *You know better.* Get off the throne, your highness!"

Most of all, love says, "Yes!" to God. When it's hard. When it's scary. When it can't see how this could possibly work. It believes all things, hopes all things, and endures all things.

Love delights in seeking its Saviour.

In truth, our "Bible study" is not about the Bible at all.

It's about Jesus.

If we truly love Him, our Bible study will be precious and sweet. Has your Bible study become routine and dry? Perhaps you need to return to your First Love. If we love Jesus with all our heart, we can find great joy in time spent in His Word. Let's choose to love Him and seek Him in the Word with all our heart!

CHAPTER 6
Scripture Memory

During the Vietnam War, a young American pilot named Howard Rutledge was promoted to the rank of Commander. He became the Executive Officer of the Fighter Squadron 191 of the US Navy. While flying a mission over North Vietnam on November 28, 1965, his plane was hit by anti-aircraft fire. He bailed out just seconds before his F-8 Crusader exploded into flames. God had spared his life in a dramatic way.

Landing in a Vietnamese village, Howard was surrounded by angry villagers and threatened with execution. But the village commissar intervened and transported him to Hanoi. Howard was held as a POW, enduring filth, torture, and isolation. He later wrote of God's guidance and protection. God answered the prayers of thousands of people who prayed for his safe return.

At this point in his life, Howard was not a faithful Christian. Although his childhood was filled with the blessings of Sunday School and church, he had long neglected church, faith, and the Lord. Now, in the darkness and despair of a Vietnamese POW camp, he was hungry for spiritual things. "During those longer periods of enforced reflection, it became so much easier to separate the important from the trivial, the worthwhile from the waste... Now the sights and sounds and smells of death were all around me. My hunger for spiritual food soon outdid my hunger for a steak. Now I wanted to talk about God and Christ and the church...It took prison to show me how empty life is without God."

Howard searched his memory for the songs, stories, and Scripture verses of his childhood education. He sang as many hymns as he could remember from memory. When he had reached 36 hymns, he was lying in bed when a terrific thunderstorm cut off the power. Listening to the torrents of falling rain, he began to hum his 37th hymn, "There shall be showers of blessing..." Howard's return to the Lord was not a solitary pursuit. His fellow POWs were also thinking of God and returning to their roots of faith. When they had brief moments of communication, they would remind each other of songs, Bible verses, and Bible stories.

In his book, *In the Presence of Mine Enemies*, Howard later wrote, "I never dreamed that I would spend almost seven years (five in solitary confinement) in a prison in North Vietnam or that thinking about one memorized verse could make the whole day bearable…" During long days of solitary confinement, he developed a routine of exercise, cleaning, and devotions. He recognized the value of the many Scripture verses he had memorized and clung to them as a beacon of hope in the dark, desperate POW camp. Leaning on God's strength, Howard endured the hardships and was released in 1973.

Although most of us will never face the horrors Howard endured, his experiences demonstrate in a concrete way the deep value of Scripture memorization. When Howard memorized verse after verse as a child, he had no idea that they would make it possible for him to survive a POW camp. God's Word gave him the hope, courage, and strength he needed so desperately. It can do the same for us. Let's memorize Scripture and learn to wield its power in our own lives.

3 Levels of Memorization

Scripture memory can be done at three different levels. We can memorize verses, chapters, and even whole books. What are the benefits of each level?

Memorizing a Verse

Memorizing single verses is the perfect place to start. If you have never memorized before, ask your pastor for a list of key verses to memorize first. As you develop confidence and skill, memorizing will become easier. You will be amazed at what you can remember!

Also, working at the verse level works well for memorizing groups of verses on one topic. If you want to memorize verses on the tongue, or music, or humility, you can search for verses that specifically address that topic. If you are struggling with a certain sin, find verses to help you battle temptation. To get started, type your keyword into a Bible concordance or online Bible. Choose five verses, and write them on one or two index cards. Work on memorizing them as a group. After you memorize the first two, make a connection between them. To do this, repeat the last phrase of the first verse and then the first few phrases of the second verse. Do this for each connection. Then, you will be able to recite them together from memory.

One group of verses that every Christian should memorize is the Romans Road. This collection gathers key verses to explain salvation. It includes verses on man's need, God's solution in Christ, and man's response. Although there are variations on it, here is a standard list of the main verses.

Romans 3:23, 3:10, 5:12, 6:23, 5:8, 10:9, 10:13, 5:1

It may also include Ephesians 2:8-9, John 14:6, and, of course, John 3:16.

We recommend learning the Romans Road as a fabulous witnessing tool. We need to "be ready always to give an answer to every man that asketh you a reason of the hope that is in you…" (1 Peter 3:15) Learning gospel-focused verses is a key strategy in our preparation to witness.

Memorizing a Chapter

Memorizing a whole chapter helps you understand context and doctrine. As you memorize the verses, your mind will start to recognize connections and themes in the chapter. If you study the chapter as you memorize it, you can gain a deeper level of understanding for its concepts.

One of the amazing benefits of memorizing a whole chapter is this. It gives you the ability to "read" the Bible when it's not in your hands. If you are an auditory learner, you can turn on a mental "audio Bible" of a memorized chapter. Without active involvement, you can hear the chapter being read aloud in your mind. If you are a visual learner, your mind may show you a picture of each verse, and you can "read" it mentally. Other types of learners may experience Bible memory in different ways. No matter what your learning style is, memorizing a whole chapter offers a whole new level of familiarity with the Bible. It builds your knowledge and memorization skills so you can memorize more with less effort.

Here are a few recommended chapters to start memorizing.
Psalm 1 contrasts the righteous, blessed man with the wicked (it has only 6 verses!)
Psalm 23 is a classic psalm about God's care and provision for us
Psalm 46 speaks in beautiful imagery of God's power, protection, and presence.
Philippians 4 offers key principles for the Christian life.
Matthew 5, though long, is so worth it! This is the first chapter of Jesus' Sermon on the Mount.
First Corinthians 13, known as "the love chapter," describes *agape*, the Greek term for authentic, sacrificial love.
James 1 gives encouragement for trials and points to God as the Source of wisdom and every good gift.

Romans 8 is a rock to cling to in the storms of life. It describes God's work in our lives—accepting us in Christ, justifying us, meeting our needs, and loving us unconditionally.

Memorizing a Book

Memorizing a whole book is a wonderful investment of your time. If you know the whole book, you can better understand its argument, tone, and themes. Exposing your mind to so much of the Word will help you clearly understand key doctrines and principles. As you study a book, you gain a "bird's-eye" view of God's Word. You begin to understand the audience and their needs. And you notice how the author built on common ground of faith, culture, and values to reach his readers. Working through a book will deepen your comprehension of Scripture significantly.

Another benefit of memorizing an entire book is that it gives you an entire storehouse of memorized Scripture. You will have many more verses that you can share with others, meditate on, and use as offensive weapons against temptation! Memorizing so much Scripture will renew your mind. It will increase your love for God's Word. Also, you can recite the Bible while looking people in the eye. This is much more powerful than simply reading the verses from your Bible. Memorizing a whole book(or even a whole chapter) is a fantastic ministry tool. It can inspire others, imprint an unforgettable memory on their hearts, and motivate them to memorize the Word as well.

You may find the very idea of memorizing a *whole book* overwhelming. Let us assure you—it is definitely possible! The secret to memorizing a book is dividing it into bite-size chunks. If you create a realistic plan and timeline, you can do it! Based on your memorizing ability and how much free time you are willing to commit, how many verses can you memorize per week? Calculate how many verses are in the whole book, and divide it by your weekly number. After adding a few weeks of flex room to your answer, you should have the number of weeks it will take you to memorize the book. Always memorize using verse numbers for easier retention and transitions.

Quick Tips for Memorization

As you memorize verses, try several techniques to discover which are most effective for you. If you are a **visual learner**, try writing out the verse several times. Or you can draw a sketch of key concepts and words. If you are an **auditory learner**, read the verse aloud several times. After becoming familiar with it, try reciting it while looking away. Work to be able to say it without looking. If you are a **music person**, you can make a simple melody to go with the words. You can find Youtube videos of Scripture verses set to music. Learning verses paired with music can be extremely helpful in both initial learning and retention.

Learn to divide and conquer. Split up the verse into its phrases. First, memorize the reference plus the first phrase. Next, say all of that plus the second phrase. Continue until you can say the whole verse. If it's a really long verse, you can memorize the phrases separately. Be sure to build strong connections between phrases by saying/writing them together.

Write out verses on 3 x 5 index cards, and place them in convenient locations. You can post them on your bathroom mirror (what else do you have to think about when you're brushing your teeth? ☺), tape one to your dashboard, and post a few above the kitchen sink. When you see them, you can easily review them.

Memorizing Scripture is an investment you will never regret. If you memorize Scripture, it will be a source of power, strength, and encouragement in your life.

Reaping the Blessings of God's Word

In Psalm 1, God describes for us the blessed man (or woman).

> Blessed is the man that walketh not in the counsel of the ungodly, nor standeth in the way of sinners, nor sitteth in the seat of the scornful. But his delight is in the law of the Lord; and in his law doth he meditate day and night. And he shall be like a tree planted by the rivers of water, that bringeth forth his fruit in his season; his leaf also shall not wither; and whatsoever he doeth shall prosper.

Blessed simply means happy. If we truly love God, we can find great happiness in reading His love letters to us. We will cherish His Words and hide them in our hearts. If we approach the Word as a treasure chest, we can discover gems of truth and the vast richness of His character. In every page, we discover more of His goodness and grace. As we seek Jesus in the Word, our devotions become rich, meaningful, and fresh. The Holy Spirit opens the Scriptures to us and teaches us new things. We encounter new concepts and build a deeper understanding of the truths we know. Our search for wisdom and understanding leads us to His feet. There, we kneel in worship, thanksgiving, and sweet adoration of the One who is utterly worthy.

In Jeremiah 15:16, the prophet writes, "Thy words were found, and I did eat them; and thy word was unto me the joy and rejoicing of mine heart: for I am called by thy name, O Lord God of hosts." As we read and memorize God's Word, we will grow to delight in it more and more. It will nourish our hearts, build our faith, and strengthen our love for God. The

Word will convict us of sin and cause us to have deep gratitude for His forgiveness and mercy. It offers hope and time-tested battle plans to overcome sin and live victoriously in Christ.

As we memorize the Word of God, we will encounter Him in all His glory and greatness. What greater reward can we ask? With the psalmist, let us pray, "Open thou mine eyes, that I may behold wondrous things out of thy law." (Psalm 119:18) Let's invest time in memorizing His Word and delight in the wondrous things we discover.

CHAPTER 7

Seeking Him in Meditation

"The reason we come away so cold from reading the Word is because we do not warm ourselves at the fire of meditation."
-John Owen

In November of 1628, a son was born to an impoverished English family in the tiny village of Elstow. Growing up, he received a limited education at the local school. As a young boy, his life was characterized by deceit, blasphemy, and feet that ran quickly toward evil. However, the lad was unusually disturbed by dreams about the torments of hell. At the tender age of sixteen, he was conscripted into the army and fought in the first period of the English Civil War. After three years of service, he left the army to return to his native village. Apprenticing with his father, he learned the family trade and set up shop. As a country artisan, he had no leisure or money to spend on books. He quickly lost what limited reading ability he had gained.

When he married at the age of 21, his wife brought into her new home a dowry of only two Puritan books. Her books were Arthur Dent's *The Plain Man's Pathway to Heaven* and Lewis Bayly's *The Practice of Piety*. With her help, he learned to read again. Those books gave him a glimmer of light and hope. Though he had wandered far off the path of righteousness, he still yearned for lasting peace. The Holy Spirit worked in his heart over the next four years, and he found peace and forgiveness at last at the foot of the cross.

Soon, God gave him a friend and mentor, Pastor John Gifford of Bedford. Under his discipleship, the young convert grew rapidly in faith. Feeling a call to preach, he became a popular lay preacher. He spent much time walking in the countryside and meditating on the Word of God. Despite his meager education, this man became the author of one of the most enduring classics of the English language.

From the pen of a humble tinker came the classic *Pilgrim's Progress.* Its author was John Bunyan. Besides this monumental work, John also published new books almost non-stop for thirty years. How did an untaught tinker produce a literary masterpiece such as *Pilgrim's Progress*?

First, John Bunyan's path to salvation was anything but easy. *Pilgrim's Progress* was born out of firsthand knowledge of the battle raging for the souls of men. Bunyan struggled with heavy guilt, serious doubts, and fear of the just wrath of God. When he found peace with God through Christ, his relief and sense of freedom were far deeper than those of the average Christian. Since he had been forgiven much, he loved much. He understood the trials and torments of a soul far from the Lord. Bunyan sought to illuminate the path to light, freedom, and victory. He offered hope to the struggling and pointed his readers to the riches of God's grace.

Second, John invested many hours in meditating on the Scriptures. The Bible was his textbook, and the Holy Spirit his Teacher. His was not a casual or haphazard pursuit. To him, the Scriptures were bread to eat, water to drink, and air to breathe. He grew to love and know the Book, and through his study, its divine Author. The Book uplifted, illuminated, and educated his mind. How did John become such a writer? In Psalm 119:98-99, the psalmist explains, "Thou through thy commandments hast made me wiser than mine enemies: for they are ever with me. I have more understanding than all my teachers: for thy testimonies are my meditation."

John did not search the Scriptures alone. His education was not marked by lonely struggle through thorn bushes and shadows. To guide his study, Bunyan had the greatest Teacher of all, the Holy Spirit. In John 10:26, Jesus told his disciples, "But the Comforter, which is the Holy Ghost, whom the Father will send in my name, he shall teach you all things, and bring all things to your remembrance, whatsoever I have said unto you." The Holy Spirit opened the Scriptures to Bunyan and revealed Christ in all His glory. Precept upon precept, line upon line, Bunyan grew in wisdom and understanding. He developed a keen understanding of man's problems and God's answers.

Coming from the school of the Holy Spirit, is it any wonder than John Bunyan wrote *Pilgrim's Progress*? What would happen, I wonder, if more Christians devoted their free time to prayerful meditation of God's Word? It starts with you and me. Let's make serious meditation a daily habit and ask God to guide us into all truth.

To prepare your heart...
Carve out ten or fifteen minutes of uninterrupted time. Set your phone to airplane mode. Find a quiet, calm place to be alone with God. Grab your Bible, a notebook or index card, and a pen or pencil. To prepare your heart, clear up any outstanding sins by asking God's forgiveness for them. Bring any worries or stresses to God and give them to Him. Ask God to open your eyes so you can see Him through His Word. Choose a verse, and copy it down on your index card or notebook.

Let's dive in...
Choose a starting method. Here are several methods we've found helpful.

ABC method
This method was developed by Dr. Nell Collins.
ABC stands for Attitude, Behaviour, and Communication. First, ask yourself what this passage teaches about God. What are His attitudes and thoughts? What does He do? What has He said? Next, apply this to your life. What specific instructions does the verse give us?
Attitude: What attitudes should you have? How and what should you think?
Behaviour: What should you do?
Communication: What should you say—both to the Lord and to people around you?
Be as specific as possible. You will benefit much more if you can apply the truth you learn to situations you are facing today.

Philippians 4:8 Questions
In Philippians 4:8, the apostle Paul commands us to think about topics that meet eight criteria. Search for the following in your verse. They can describe either the Lord or people.
What is true (accurate, reliable, facts)?
What is just (fair)?
What is pure (untainted by the evil of this world)?
What is lovely?
What is of good report (having a good reputation, glorifying God)?
What virtues can you find? (The seven traditionally Christian virtues are faith, hope, charity, fortitude, justice, temperance, and prudence.)
What is praiseworthy (worthy of honour, excellent)?
Record what you discover. Ask yourself, "How can I model my life after these criteria? What can I do today to be more just, honest, pure, lovely, etc.?"

Word emphasis method
This method is best for short to medium length verses. For example, take the verse Psalm 23:1.

"The Lord is my shepherd; I shall not want." Consider one word at a time.

The: The singular article reminds me that there is only one true God. He alone rules Heaven and earth. He is without equal.

Lord: This word is translated from the Hebrew *Yahweh*, meaning "Lord" or "Master." The Jews viewed this Name as so holy that they would not pronounce it. Instead, they would read it as "Adonai," which meant a human lord or master. (You can look up the original words used in a lexicon—either paper or online.)

is: A being verb, this reminds us of God's eternal life. He had no birth, and He will have no end.

my: This possessive adjective reminds us that, if we have accepted Christ, He is ours. We can claim Him as our own! He is present and active in our lives.

Shepherd: A shepherd cares for his sheep, provides for their needs, and loves them unconditionally from birth to death. Doesn't the Lord do the same for us?

I: Now the focus turns to me. Because He is my Shepherd, what will I do?

shall: A helping verb, this signifies decision and resolve. I *will* stick to my decision.

not: This adverb modifies the next word.

want: Here, the meaning of *want* is to lack or be short of. Because God is my Shepherd, I will not lack anything. He will meet every need with His all-sufficient grace. I will choose not to worry about the future. I will choose to trust my Shepherd.

You don't need to write all this out, but this is the mental process you would use. Record your conclusions and discoveries.

Joseph Hall method:
This method can be used for a word or concept within a verse. Answer as many of the following questions as you can.
1. What is it (define and/or describe what it is)?
2. What are its divisions or parts?
3. What causes it?
4. What does it cause, i.e., its fruits and effects?
5. What is its place, location, or use?
6. What are its qualities and attachments?
7. What is contrary, contradictory, or different to it?
8. What compares to it?
9. What are its titles or names?
10. What are the testimonies or examples of Scripture about it?

LEARN method
This method focuses on questions about God.
Likeness: What descriptions of God can you find?

Emotions: What emotions of God are revealed? What does He love? What does He hate?
Actions: What does God do? Why does He do it?
Revelation: What truth and wisdom does God give us?
Names: What Names of God are given? Research them for more detail.
After you find some information, ask yourself what impact it should have on your life. Can you reflect the characteristics of the Lord in your choices today?

Cross-References
If your Bible has cross-references, you will notice superscript letters like this[a] to indicate cross-references. Look for a center column or endnotes at the bottom of the page, and locate that letter. Look up the verse(s) listed with it, and consider the similarities between the verses. What phrase or keywords occur in both verses? What additional information does the second verse provide? This method can help you study a concept or word in more detail.

SAVED method:
This acronym stands for the following things to look for in a verse.
Sins to avoid?
Actions to take?
Virtues to develop?
Examples to follow or avoid?
Descriptions of God(character, ways, words)?

Opposites method
State the opposite form of the verse. If your verse was "The Lord is my Shepherd; I shall not want," you would write, "The Lord is not my Shepherd; I shall want." That could lead you to explore the connection between God being our Shepherd and our needs being met.

Or, you can choose a key word and look up its antonyms(opposites) and synonyms(similar words). Compare the key word to the other words you find. Try to describe it as clearly as you can. Ask God to help you understand it better. How can you apply this word in your life?

Making it personal...
As you meditate on Scripture, the Holy Spirit will reveal truth to you. How should you respond to the truth you encounter in God's Word?

Choose to Obey Him
Imagine that the Bible is like a vast hallway with a full-length mirror running down one wall. As you look into the mirror, the Holy Spirit will show you a glimpse of who you really are. Thankfully, He sheds only a little bit of light

at a time on our sin nature. If we saw the "Me Monster" in broad daylight, we'd probably pass out on the spot. That is one ugly creature! Instead, He spotlights just a small section—perhaps a habit to change, a belief to apply in our daily walk, or a trap to avoid. When the Holy Spirit speaks to us in this way, we have two choices.

1) Pretend we didn't hear Him, and run really, really fast in the opposite direction.
2) Swallow our pride, and say, "Yes, Lord. I will obey You."

Which choice would bring us closer to Him? If we are serious about seeking Him, we will choose to obey the truth He reveals to us.

The apostle James describes the futility of receiving God's Word but not obeying it.

> For if any be a hearer of the word, and not a doer, he is like unto a man beholding his natural face in a glass: For he beholdeth himself, and goeth his way, and straightway forgetteth what manner of man he was. But whoso looketh into the perfect law of liberty, and continueth therein, he being not a forgetful hearer, but a doer of the work, this man shall be blessed in his deed. (James 1:23-25)

Will you be a doer of the Word or simply a hearer? God only promises blessings to the doers of the Word. Let's squash the protests of the flesh and boldly obey His Word. Obedience is well worth it!

Worship Him

In our mirror analogy, where does the light come from? Does it not come from the glory of God? Though God has given us some light on earth, how small and feeble is our knowledge of the true Light! We are like children emerging from a tiny, dark, dirty closet into a vast atrium filled with glorious light. In the light, we shyly notice that our fingernails are dirty. Then we see that our hands are dirty, too—our feet are filthy, our clothes stained—why, our whole bodies need a thorough cleansing! How could we not see this before? Standing in the radiant light, we begin to see things as they really are. And we begin to see the Lord as we have never seen Him before.

Could we have dreamed or even imagined that He was so precious, so good, and so sweet? Ah, this is what He meant when He offered, "O taste and see that the Lord is good: blessed is the man that trusteth in him." (Psalm 34:8) As the Holy Spirit opens our eyes, rich colours and sparkling rubies of truth flash from line after line. We glimpse the love of God for us in all its depth and height and wonder. To sacrifice His only Son to a rebellious people, to taste the suffering and pain of a sin-sick race, to kneel and whisper, "Not My will, but Thine, be done." Here is love, deeper than the ocean, vaster than the universe, and more enduring than time itself! Struck with our own unworthiness, we are overwhelmed by the reality of God's grace. Can we do anything but kneel and worship?

When we see Jesus in the pages of Scripture, worship should be the first joyful response of our hearts. "I knew You were good, but I didn't realize You were *this good!*" The deeper we search the Scriptures, the more clearly we see His face. From the deserts of Genesis to the celestial visions of Revelation, it is *His Story*. Feeding on the Scriptures increases our love for Christ. We stand amazed as Jesus appears to Joshua. Drawn sword in hand, He tells Joshua to take off his shoes since he is now on holy ground. We watch Him tenderly take the hand of Jairus' daughter and bring her back to life. We weep with Peter as the cock crows and Jesus turns to look at him. We go fishing with the heartsick disciples. After a night of catching nothing, we see a man standing on the shore. He calls out, "Cast the net on the right side of the ship, and ye shall find." (John 21:6) We throw out our nets, and they are so heavy we can't drag them into the boat! With John, we whisper in wonder, "It is the Lord." (John 21:7) Jesus calls us to shore and invites us to partake of His food. In Scripture, we taste the goodness of God and are filled.

If we meditate on the Word diligently, God promises us a rich reward. "But we all, with open face beholding as in a glass the glory of the Lord, are changed into the same image from glory to glory, even as by the Spirit of the Lord." (2 Corinthians 3:18) His light spills into our hearts and lives, and we are changed forever. What a promise! Meditating on the Word will change us into His Image, which is infinitely beautiful. Let's meditate diligently and delight in seeking Him in the Word!

CHAPTER 8

Obedience: The Test of Love

If ye love me, keep my commandments.
—Jesus, in John 14:15

As we learn to seek Jesus through the spiritual disciplines, the truths we learn about Him spill over into our daily lives. When we meditate on the Scriptures, the Holy Spirit identifies specific areas in which we fall short of the glory of God. He convicts us of sin in our hearts, words, and actions. He calls us to a higher standard. If we obey the Holy Spirit, He gradually shapes the rough clay of our lives into pristine vessels of glory and honour. Personal obedience is the only pathway to authentic spiritual growth.

Also, growing closer to Jesus hinges on our obedience. Our depth of relationship has a direct correlation to our obedience (or lack thereof). "Jesus answered and said unto him, If a man love me, he will keep my words: and my Father will love him, and we will come unto him, and make our abode with him." (John 14:23) Knowing Jesus and loving Jesus are inseparably connected with obeying Him. If you want to know Jesus more deeply and love Jesus more fervently, you must begin by obeying Him.

Authentic Obedience

God calls us to authentic obedience. This obedience flows from an attitude of *submission* to God's will. Often, we use the terms "submission" and "surrender" interchangeably. However, one preacher noted an important distinction between them. "Surrender" means to give up yourself to the power of another. But surrender is not final. In wartime, soldiers who have "surrendered" have not given up their allegiance to their nation. They have not given up the possibility of escape or hopes of eventual victory. If given the right opportunity, they will attack their captors, escape, and march into battle again. Surrender implies a temporary submission to an authority.

In contrast, to "submit" is to give up yourself to another *without* any hope or desire to escape. To submit means to bow both the knee and the heart.

When we truly submit to God, we give Him both the steering wheel of our life and the remote control of our mind. We choose to honour Him in both our outward actions and our inward thoughts and desires. We submit to His wishes—not only today, but also tomorrow, and next year, and for the indefinite future.

If we have a heart submitted to Jesus, obedience is simple and joyful. But, if we have only surrendered temporarily, we will struggle to obey Him. A temporary surrender is not enough. To seek Jesus, we must submit ourselves as a living sacrifice. (Romans 12:1)

As we submit to Jesus, He transforms our hearts. Looking at life through fresh eyes, we discover joy in obeying Him. We give thanks for the work He sets before us, the light He shines on our path, and the grace He supplies every day. When we have a thankful spirit, obedience is delightful. Joy is both the fruit and the hallmark of authentic obedience.

Perhaps you have heard the saying, "Obedience is obeying immediately, exactly, and cheerfully." Many godly parents teach this motto to their children. From it, we can glean an easily overlooked truth. Obedience is obeying *immediately*. How many times has the Holy Spirit directed you to a specific action, yet you delayed? How many times have we ignored His voice? Have we grieved the Spirit of God by our disobedience? He does not say, "Do this whenever you get a chance, or when you feel like it." Instead, He commands, "Do this NOW."

Obeying God "later" is actually not obeying Him at all. Delaying our obedience means changing God's schedule. It is telling God, "I know better than You, and I want to do this later, not now." In contrast, authentic obedience obeys God immediately.

Also, authentic obedience influences our decision-making process. When we are not walking in obedience, we make decisions without seeking Him. We may ask our family, friends, and even pastor for advice, but we neglect to seek His direction. Or we may follow the wisdom of this world, which is faulty and unreliable. And our knowledge is limited, and our perspective skewed by our sin nature. The prophet Jeremiah wrote, "O Lord, I know that the way of man is not in himself: it is not in man that walketh to direct his steps." (Jer. 10:23) Without God's wisdom, we cannot make wise decisions. James 1:5 tells us, "If any of you lack wisdom, let him ask of God, that giveth to all men liberally, and upbraideth not; and it shall be given him." God has storehouses overflowing with eternal wisdom, freely available to all who ask. We should both ask for His wisdom to make decisions and strength to obey His will.

When we show authentic obedience, we bow the knee before God's authority. We submit completely, trusting His wisdom instead of following our own agenda. As we obey, the joy of Jesus brightens and colours our days. We learn to respond immediately to the Holy Spirit's direction. Most importantly, we practice seeking God for direction in decision-making. Authentic obedience means obeying God from the heart, and, through that process, knowing His heart.

The Danger of Partial Obedience

Partial obedience is toxic to our spiritual life. Under its influence, we think that we are being obedient to God. But this insidious poison halts all possibility of growth. It is a stench in God's nostrils and a stumblingblock to fellow Christians. What is partial obedience? How does it wrap its sinewy tentacles around our hearts? Let's examine this danger more closely. As you read on, be brave enough to search your life and heart for any traces of partial obedience.

Partial obedience means obeying part of God's commands, but not all of them. While paying lip service to God, we do not yield our lives completely to Him. We are willing to obey commands that seem reasonable and safe. But we refuse to obey God when He calls us to take a leap of faith. Also, we reserve certain rooms of our heart for private sins. On their doors, we post a large "Keep Out!" sign. After all, God can't expect perfection, can He? We just want to have a little fun. With partial obedience, we insist on running our lives as we see fit. We build our plans on personal desires, ambitions, and goals—without thought or regard for God's will.

Partial obedience is often connected with selective hearing. We ignore any commands which seem unpleasant, uncertain, or impossibly difficult. Selective hearing can include ignoring parts of the Bible. We may "forget" His instructions, warnings, and counsel. Perhaps we even acknowledge that God has spoken to our hearts, but we "modify" His plans to suit our wishes. After all, we know better than God, right? His plan would never work! Selective hearing is terribly easy to do, but it is a slap in God's face. Thousands of angels serve Him day and night. Heavenly creatures worship His holiness in never-ending anthems. Wind and waves, sun and moon—yes, every element of nature—obey His Word and fulfill His wishes to the letter. Yet frail humans dare to ignore His voice or even say, "I didn't hear You the first time." What madness, what folly is this! May we never be guilty of selective hearing.

Sometimes, we even try to escape the voice of God through distractions. We busy ourselves with our career, our family, and even our ministry. We rush through our devotional time and hold Jesus at arm's length. We fill our lives with noise—loud, pressing, insistent noise. And, too often, we succeed in distracting ourselves from the Holy Spirit's gentle whisper. We content ourselves with partial obedience.

Often, we make excuses for our partial obedience. We write detailed, convincing excuse notes for why we can't obey God. Here are a few possible excuses you could adapt to your situation.

"God doesn't really expect me to do that. He knows I've had a difficult background."

"I can't help the way I am. This [sin] is just part of my personality."

"I don't want to get too religious. What would my friends and family think?"

"At least I'm not as bad as some people. Look at the mess they've made of their lives! I'm really doing quite well."

"Lord, I will do that when I get a chance. I'm just too busy right now."

"I'm too young / too old. Nobody would listen to me."

"I don't have the experience/ talents/ resources for the job. I just know I'd be a failure."

If we examine the heart behind these excuses, we discover an unpleasant truth. Every single excuse is based on the lie, "I know better than God does." However, Romans 11:33 deals a deathblow to this statement. "O the depth of the riches both of the wisdom and knowledge of God! how unsearchable are his judgments, and his ways past finding out!" When we are tempted to make excuses, we should remind ourselves of God's infinite wisdom. We must decide to trust and obey Him completely.

Partial obedience will cause us to receive *partial blessing*. Instead of receiving the full riches of God's goodness, we will miss out on His best. Consider how King Saul lost his kingdom. After only two years as king, Saul chose three thousand men for an army. After a successful raid against the Philistine garrison, he called all Israel together to war against the Philistines. In 1 Samuel 13, Saul and his army waited seven days for the prophet Samuel to arrive. He had to offer a sacrifice before they marched into battle. Fearful, the people begin to scatter, abandoning Saul. Desperate, Saul orders his servants to prepare offerings for sacrifice. He offers a burnt offering to God, in blatant disobedience of the Mosaic law. According to that law, only anointed priests, descended from Aaron's line, were permitted to offer sacrifices.

As Saul finished offering the burnt offering, the prophet Samuel arrived. He asked one simple question, "What hast thou done?" (1 Samuel 13:11) Saul offers a complex, pious-sounding excuse. The people were scattered,

Samuel didn't show up, and the Philistines assembled for battle. "Therefore said I, The Philistines will come down now upon me to Gilgal, and I have not made supplication unto the LORD: I forced myself therefore, and offered a burnt offering." (1 Sam. 13:12) Hear the sorrow and disappointment in Samuel's rebuke:

> And Samuel said to Saul, Thou hast done foolishly: thou hast not kept the commandment of the Lord thy God, which he commanded thee: for now would the Lord have established thy kingdom upon Israel for ever. But now thy kingdom shall not continue: the Lord hath sought him a man after his own heart, and the Lord hath commanded him to be captain over his people, because thou hast not kept that which the Lord commanded thee. (1 Samuel 13:13-14)

Saul obeyed God partially. He went out to fight against the enemies of God. He assembled his people to battle. He waited seven days for Samuel. Until the seventh day, Saul was obedient to God. But he overstepped his boundaries by offering a sacrifice that God had not authorized. He acted foolishly in the heat of the moment. Because of this sin, Saul's kingdom was given to another, a man after God's own heart. For the remaining twenty-five years of his reign, Saul lived in the shadow of Samuel's prophecy. Saul knew that his son Jonathan would never sit on his throne. He would never leave a royal dynasty. This disobedience was the beginning of the end for Saul. He struggled with depression, demonic attacks, and bitter envy. When David rose to prominence, Saul became envious. He even tried to murder David several times and hunted him down in the wilderness. At the age of seventy-two, Saul died a lowly death in battle against the Philistines.

When Saul became impatient and made a "minor" choice to disobey God, he never dreamed that he would lose his kingdom because of it. He did not foresee the impact his choice would have—not only on his life, but also on the lives of his children and grandchildren. Because Saul obeyed God only part of the time, he lost so much. He lost his kingdom, his good name, and his peace. He lost the most precious treasure he had—the blessing of God on his life.

Like Saul, do we live in partial obedience? Do we choose to obey God only when it is convenient? Do we ignore some of the commands of God and follow our hearts instead? If we choose partial obedience, we will halt our spiritual growth. We will miss out on many of God's blessings for our life. Don't settle for partial obedience. Purpose to obey completely, no matter what the cost.

Rewards for Obedience

If we pursue authentic obedience in our lives, God will reward us richly. Here are just a few of God's amazing rewards for obedience.

1) Abundant Joy

Authentic obedience always produces the fruit of joy in our lives. Jesus told His disciples, "If ye keep my commandments, ye shall abide in my love…These things have I spoken unto you, that my joy might remain in you, and that your joy might be full." (John 15:10-11) God doesn't want His children to trudge through life with long, gloomy faces and heavy hearts. He didn't save us so we could be the "First World martyrs," adhering to a lengthy list of rules and always worrying about being good enough. That would completely miss the point. God's heart for us is that we obey Him, know Him, and love Him. As we do this, He will open our eyes to see life through the lens of His joy.

Often, the enemy tempts us to disobey God by promising pleasure and satisfaction. But the pleasures of sin are hollow and temporary. Sin robs us of the lasting pleasure to be found in God's presence. Only obedience from the heart will give us true joy.

2) Rest

As Christ said in John 15:10, "If ye keep my commandments, ye shall abide in my love; even as I have kept my Father's commandments, and abide in his love." When we disobey God, we cannot experience rest and peace in our souls. Even if we can squash our conscience's protests, we lose our capacity to rest. Niggling worries begin a merry-go-round in our minds. Guilt slips in the door of our hearts. Fear reaches its icy fingers into our soul. What is wrong? We have chosen sin over God, rebellion over loyalty. If we repent and ask His forgiveness, we can return to a place of rest under His wings.

Even in trying and stressful circumstances, obedience gives us rest. If we obey, we know that we have done our part. We can leave the outcome in God's capable hands. All He requires is that we obey—not that we solve world poverty, foretell the future, or fix our spouses. Let's simply obey and find a place of true rest…in His loving care.

3) Continued Guidance

Elisabeth Elliot said it well, "Does it make sense to pray for guidance about the future if we are not obeying in the thing that lies before us today?…Rest assured: Do what God tells you to do now, and, depend upon it, you will be shown what to do next."

Psalm 37:23 gives us God's promise, "The steps of a good man are ordered by the Lord: and he delighteth in his way." A good man faithfully obeys the Lord. As he does so, God will direct his steps. Our obedience today is vital if we want to have God's guidance tomorrow.

4) A Deeper Relationship with Jesus
The ultimate reward for obedience is knowing Jesus more deeply. People who disobey and rebel against God tend to view Him as a distant, cold-hearted judge. They may even imagine that He likes to condemn, chasten, and punish mankind. Perhaps He is actually mean and cruel, not compassionate and just. It is much easier to excuse our disobedience if God is not really good, if He is warped and cold-blooded, if He is a corrupt Ruler. However, we know that God is not any of the above. The enemy loves to throw mud at God's character and provide convenient excuses for disobedience. Don't believe his accusations.

In truth, obeying God is like stepping over a threshold into a lush courtyard of rich greenery, fruit-laden trees, and singing birds. In this courtyard, we meet the greatest Friend we will ever have. We linger with the merciful Saviour who washed our sins away. And we kneel in adoration before the Father who loved us with an eternal love. In the courtyard, we revel in the presence of our Lord. He delights in us and encourages our hearts to continue obeying Him. Sometimes, He opens our eyes to recognize the wisdom and goodness of His will. Other times, He asks us, "Do you trust Me?" and challenges us to obedience. God's commands do not always make sense before we obey them. After we obey, we grasp more deeply that God really does know best!

Through obedience, we draw near to the heart of God. We are blessed by His joy, His rest, and His continued guidance. God delights in rewarding His obedient children.

The Test of Your Heart
The test of obedience to God pulls aside the curtain on our hearts. Partial obedience and disobedience reveal a heart that loves itself more than Jesus. Authentic obedience reveals a heart that truly loves Jesus. Do we obey Jesus consistently? Is our obedience joyful and eager, or reluctant and half-hearted? Do we love Jesus most, or do we love ourselves most? Our actions reveal what is in our heart. Authentic obedience plays a pivotal role in seeking Jesus.

In the words of Jesus Himself, "He that hath my commandments, and keepeth them, *he it is that loveth me*: and he that loveth me shall be loved of my Father, and I will love him, and will manifest myself to him." (John 10:21, emphasis added)

CHAPTER 9

Blessed Are the Pure in Heart

And what kind of habitation pleases God?
What must our natures be like before he can feel at home within us?
He asks nothing but a pure heart and a single mind.
He asks no rich paneling, no rugs from the Orient,
no art treasures from afar.
He desires but sincerity, transparency, humility, and love.
He will see to the rest.
-A. W. Tozer

Since the moment of salvation, the Holy Spirit indwells our hearts. As A. W. Tozer stated, He does not ask for mahogany paneling, ancient Oriental rugs, and costly art treasures. Instead, He asks for a pure heart and a single mind. In Matthew 5:8, Jesus said, "Blessed are the pure in heart: for they shall see God." Since He is absolutely holy, God keeps the richness and glory of His presence veiled. At the door to His sanctuary, we face a searching test. At that moment, are we pure in heart? We cannot pass this test with borrowed credit or secondhand righteousness. We cannot point to our stellar reputation or our glowing achievements. God searches our hearts and understands all our thoughts (1 Chronicles 28:9). If we are found lacking–if selfishness and sin have darkened our hearts–we are barred from the presence of God. We cannot look on His holiness and taste His goodness.

To enter the presence of a holy God, our hearts must be pure. How can we purify our hearts? What rooms should we tackle with mop and broom, detergent and soapy water? What principles should govern our moral choices? In this chapter, we'll discover how to cultivate pure hearts so that we, too, can see Jesus.

Our Thought Life

Purity of heart begins in our thought life. Our thoughts both reveal our current character and shape our character tomorrow. "For as he thinketh in his heart, so is he..." (Proverbs 23:7a) Moment by moment, we must choose good thoughts or evil ones. Each thought we choose influences our lives—for good or for evil. Evil thoughts turn our hearts away from God. Good thoughts produce a pure heart that loves Jesus. Our thought life is the first battle we have to win and, often, the most difficult. If we can achieve victory in our thought life, we can have victory in every other aspect of our Christian life.

In Matthew 15, the Pharisees rebuked Jesus' disciples for eating with unwashed hands. But He responded that food cannot defile anyone. He stated, "But those things which proceed out of the mouth come forth from the heart; and they defile the man. For out of the heart proceed evil thoughts, murders, adulteries, fornications, thefts, false witness, blasphemies: These are the things which defile a man: but to eat with unwashen hands defileth not a man." (Matthew 15:18-20) Unfortunately, our sin nature has a natural tendency toward evil thoughts. If we are not careful, our thoughts gravitate toward wrong thoughts. To have a pure thought life, we must recognize this tendency and resist it.

When we are tempted to think wrong thoughts, we can remember the words of Paul in 2 Corinthians 10:5. To experience victory in the Christian life, he said that we must be, "Casting down imaginations, and every high thing that exalteth itself against the knowledge of God, and bringing into captivity every thought to the obedience of Christ;" The words "cast down" mean that we must immediately subdue wrong thoughts. We cannot allow them to roam freely through our minds, stealing our hearts from God. When a thought appears, we should judge if it is good or evil. If it is evil, we should reject it immediately. Consistently rejecting wrong thoughts will become a habit and help us tremendously. Just as our words and behaviour must be submitted to the authority of Christ, our thoughts, too, must obey His authority.

As Christians, we have been given the mind of Christ. 1 Corinthians 2:16 tells us, "For who hath known the mind of the Lord, that he may instruct him? but we have the mind of Christ." Since we are in Christ, we can have victory over wrong thoughts. We can learn to replace them with godly, acceptable thoughts. How does the Bible describe good thoughts? In Philippians 4:8, Paul lists eight categories of profitable thoughts.

> Finally, brethren, whatsoever things are true, whatsoever things are honest, whatsoever things are just, whatsoever things are pure, whatsoever things are lovely, whatsoever things are of good report; if there be any virtue, and if there be any praise, think on these things.

The Bible abounds with examples of virtue, honesty, justice, purity, etc. Also, it gives us many precious promises of God and inspiring verses about Him. To cultivate good thoughts, we can start by thinking about Jesus and meditating on His Word. We can also count the blessings He showers upon us every day. Reminiscing about the paths we've travelled with Him, we can recognize His loving hand. We can memorize His Word (as we talked about in chapter 6) and recite it mentally. Also, we can find food for thought in sermons, Christian books, and the lives of great Christians throughout history. The story of Eric Liddell's triumph, the perils David Livingstone faced, and the genius of Isaac Newton can inspire us to do hard things. The classic works of the faith, such as *My Utmost for His Highest, The Practice of the Presence of God,* and *Mere Christianity,* can kindle our love for God and invigorate our minds. As we nourish our minds with these treasures, our thought life will become more fruitful, bright, and pure.

Our Music

Music shapes our minds and hearts significantly. It exerts a moral influence on us, persuading us to choose right or wrong, obedience or rebellion. Music is by no means neutral. Each song we listen to and each artist we support tips the scales of our lives toward either good or evil. Music teaches us to make certain choices. Consider some of the messages that the wrong kind of music teaches.

"If it feels good, do it."
"It doesn't matter who you hurt, as long as you're happy."
"Follow your heart."
"There is no absolute standard of morals."
"Nobody can tell you how to run your life."
"Violence toward women is acceptable and even normal."
"There is no God."

Obviously, such messages are not only false, but also dangerous. They contradict the Bible's clear revelation. The wrong kind of music appeals to our sin nature instead of our spirit. It calls us to indulge ourselves and do what is right in our own eyes. The wrong music will defile and corrupt our hearts. Beyond merely listening, it will lead us to believe and act upon its deceitful messages. Recognizing its great hazard to our spiritual health, we must reject such music.

Nevertheless, not all secular music is wrong. One genre in particular, classical music, has been embraced by many Christians for its beauty and quality. Its demand for excellence and focus on details provide excellent training for Christian musicians. In addition to classical, there are other genres of music that can fit into our playlists without corrupting our hearts. Lively marching band music, the dramatic songs of musical theatre, and barbershop quartets in sweet harmony–these are often acceptable and enjoyable. Also, folk/traditional music can fit into our standards. Traditional music, both vocal and instrumental, records the tales of ordinary men and women in the struggles and triumphs of life. It preserves the heritage of our cultures, our languages, and our families. Traditional music spans many cultures and instruments. Lilting Celtic tunes, fiery Hungarian dances, and exotic Japanese compositions–these are just a few examples of traditional music. Secular music can provide clean entertainment and enjoyment for Christians. It can also train Christian musicians to play sacred music.

Sacred music is specifically dedicated to and centred upon God. It has two goals–to worship God and to edify Christians. Unfortunately, there has been a major shift in Christian music towards imitating the techniques, methods, and sounds of worldly, immoral music. When sacred music is negatively influenced by secular music, it appeals to the flesh rather than the spirit. It offers an emotional experience instead of objective truth. Its message is watered down, simplified, and sugar-coated for popular appeal. We must ask ourselves, "Does my sacred music show any of these symptoms?" If it does, we should prayerfully look for better sacred music. There are many Christian publishers, musicians, and composers who provide and perform outstanding sacred music. Ask your pastor or church musicians for recommendations.

If we aspire to have pure hearts, we must choose our music wisely. If we seek God's wisdom and guidance, we can develop a balanced standard for our personal music choices. Your playlist will look a bit different than someone else's. God gives each of us the freedom to choose our music according to the dictates of our conscience. We can take pleasure in selected secular music and grow our skills by playing it. Our sacred music can inspire our hearts to greater holiness and love for Jesus. It can motivate us, strengthen us, and teach us eternal truth. If we build a well-chosen playlist of secular and sacred music, it will colour our days with beauty, strength, and fresh energy. With the psalmist, we will rejoice in singing a new song. "And he hath put a new song in my mouth, even praise unto our God: many shall see it, and fear, and shall trust in the LORD." (Psalm 40:3)

Our Entertainment

Unfortunately, it is becoming very difficult to find acceptable entertainment. Too often, entertainment is marked by sensuality, profanity, and ungodly values. It is often designed to promote a variety of ungodly lifestyles. One movie at a time, its goal is to transform our culture. Most entertainment today flows from a worldview that opposes God and Biblical Christianity. Instead, it embraces relative morality, the pursuit of pleasure above all else, "social justice," and postmodern values. Modern entertainment often demeans authority and attacks the Biblical roles of men and women in both their family and society.

If we as Christians accept our culture's entertainment, our hearts will be affected by it. It will desensitize us to violence, death, and the seriousness of man's sin. Pop entertainment will educate us about the evil of this world. No matter how strongly we resist its pull, ungodly entertainment always has a price tag. It does far more than steal our time away from more profitable activities. It will also cost us our innocence, mar our hope and optimism, and steal our hearts away from Jesus. In our opinion, this price tag is far too high.

When we stand before the Judgment Seat of Christ, will we have any excuse for investing hours in ungodly entertainment? How will we possibly justify its content and values before a holy God? I think we will be without excuse. But the good news is that we are not before the Judgment Seat of Christ yet. We still have the opportunity to change our entertainment choices. 1 John 3:1-2 offers us a powerful motivation to change.

> Beloved, now are we the sons of God, and it doth not yet appear what we shall be: but we know that, when he shall appear, we shall be like him; for we shall see him as he is. And every man that hath this hope in him purifieth himself, even as he is pure."

Recognizing that we will be like Christ motivates us to purify our lives today. With the Holy Spirit's help, we should evaluate our personal entertainment choices. How much time do we spend on entertainment? We may benefit from investing more time in active recreation (exercise, hobbies) and less time in passive recreation.

Also, is our entertainment acceptable in God's sight? Although they are more difficult to find, we can locate clean, family-friendly movies. There are still Christians that shine the light of Christ into the darkness of modern entertainment. Christian filmmakers, composers, and screenwriters produce films about family, faith, and the gospel. From established companies like Pure Flix and Big Idea Entertainment to indie studios like Burns and Co. Productions, Christians have stepped up to write, act in, and present quality entertainment. Faith-based films can illustrate truth through storytelling and inspire us to walk faithfully. They can also be a helpful evangelistic tool to watch with non-Christian friends and family.

We should carefully consider our entertainment options and choose wisely. In addition to movies, we should be careful about the books that we read. Many books do not honor God and promote Biblical values. We should also be careful about our social media activity. The pull of the world can be very strong. And we are influenced by peer pressure more than we may like to admit. If we want to have pure hearts, we need to be careful about everything we read, watch, and listen to. Like the psalmist, let's resolve, "I will set no wicked thing before mine eyes: I hate the work of them that turn aside; it shall not cleave to me." (Psalm 101:3)

Principles to Live By

As we seek to have a pure heart, the Holy Spirit will coach us step by step. He will point a finger at an area of our life that needs improvement. Perhaps we have familiar bad habits that prevent our spiritual growth. We may have friends to whom we must say goodbye. Or we may be involved in activities that distract us from God's plan for our lives. To obey His voice, we must make moral choices and create personal policies. What principles guide us in making moral choices?

1) We must say no to anything that enslaves us.
Paul wrote to the Corinthian church, "All things are lawful unto me, but all things are not expedient: all things are lawful for me, but I will not be brought under the power of any." (1 Cor. 6:12) As believers, we have great liberty in Christ. But we must avoid being enslaved by earthly things. For a questionable thing in your life, ask yourself the following questions.

Is this expedient? Has it helped me grow spiritually?
Am I under its power? Does it influence my decisions?
Has it claimed the love that only Jesus should have?

In Hebrews 12:1, God calls us to "...lay aside every weight, and the sin which doth so easily beset us..." We may have weights in our lives, things that enslave us. Although they are not sinful, they prevent us from running a faithful race. We must lay them aside.

2) We must not influence other Christians to sin.
In Romans 14, we read, "Let us not therefore judge one another any more: but judge this rather, that no man put a stumblingblock or an occasion to fall in his brother's way...It is good neither to eat flesh, nor to drink wine, nor any thing whereby thy brother stumbleth, or is offended, or is made weak." (Romans 14:13, 21) Although we may be able to do something with a clear conscience, our brothers and sisters in Christ may not. They may have a weaker conscience. Our unwitting example may cause them to stumble into sin. "But when ye sin so against the brethren, and wound their weak conscience, ye sin against Christ." (1 Corinthians 8:12) We should strive to be a godly example, not causing anyone to stumble.

3) We must not give unnecessary offence.

As believers, we know that the cross of Christ is an offence. As we share the message of the cross, sin, and judgment to come, people will be offended. We should not be surprised at this, for the world was also offended at Jesus' words. However, we must not cause personal offence. We may cause personal offence by a cold, critical, and unloving spirit. We may cause offence by supervising instead of serving, finding fault instead of praising, and lecturing instead of listening. 1 Corinthians 10:32 calls us to "Give none offence, neither to the Jews, nor to the Gentiles, nor to the church of God: Even as I please all men in all things, not seeking mine own profit, but the profit of many, that they may be saved." Like Paul, we should seek the salvation of others and, as much as possible, avoid giving offence.

4) We must glorify God in every action.
1 Corinthians 6:20, "For ye are bought with a price: therefore glorify God in your body, and in your spirit, which are God's." As Christians, we represent Jesus. Our work should reflect His diligence, attention to detail, and excellence. Our lips should be filled with words that please Him. Our time should be invested in worthwhile pursuits. Our resources should be managed with wise stewardship. Our attitudes should reflect His joy, peace, and faithful love.

These four principles can direct you in choosing wisely and keeping your heart pure.

Is Your Heart Pure?

As you read this chapter, perhaps God spoke to your heart about something particular. Maybe you have allowed weeds to spring up and sin to stain the purity of your heart. Or selfishness and pride may have shoved Jesus off the throne of your heart. Each of us has room to improve, to love Jesus more deeply, and to develop a more pure heart.

Even if your heart is far from purity, God offers you mercy and grace. He invites...

> Seek ye the LORD while he may be found, call ye upon him while he is near:
> Let the wicked forsake his way, and the unrighteous man his thoughts: and let him return unto the LORD, and he will have mercy upon him; and to our God, for he will abundantly pardon. (Isaiah 55:6-7)

If we forsake our sins and turn to Him, we can taste the joy of His presence again. Even if your trail to His door has been choked by weeds and draped with spiderwebs, you can return. Brush away the spiderwebs; mow down the undergrowth. Cleanse your heart and hands, and run down the trail again. "Who shall ascend into the hill of the Lord? or who shall stand in his holy place? He that hath clean hands, and a pure heart; who hath not lifted up his soul unto vanity, nor sworn deceitfully." (Psalm 24:3-4) Let's seek Jesus with a pure heart!

CHAPTER 10
Seeking Him in the Everyday

To see every leaf as painted by a Master's brush, to delight in a song that thrills your heart, to fall in adoration before the Throne—this is the joy of seeking Him in everyday life!

When God created the universe, He left divine fingerprints on everything He touched. As a result, we can catch glimpses of Him through His creation. From the spires of the mountains that touch the sky to the innocent laugh of a little child, creation teaches us the character of God. No matter where you look, God is in the everyday.

God does not limit His presence to specific locations or times. In the Old Testament, God's presence was only accessible once a year, in one physical location, by one man on earth. But the Holy Spirit now indwells every true believer. How privileged we are to have God's very presence in our hearts! When we seek God in the everyday, we can see His work in the commonplace details of life. In the daily grind, we can walk hand in hand with the most High.

Mountaintop Experiences

Too many people are looking for a mountaintop experience, a revelation of some kind. They want God to reveal Himself to them as He did for Moses on Mount Sinai or for Peter, James, and John on the Mount of Transfiguration. People want an exciting emotional experience to confirm their faith. They long for a sudden flash of light that will show them the mysteries of life and God. But God has not told us to seek a new revelation or new truth. The psalmist wrote, "For ever, O Lord, thy word is settled in heaven." (Psalm 119:89) God has already given us the light we need in His Word. Psalm 119:105 declares, "Thy word is a lamp unto my feet, and a light unto my path."

I've had the opportunity to hike up some mountains in my life. Just this past year my wife and I [Jason] made the climb up Mount Pipet in Vienne, France. Okay, so it wasn't the Rockies, the Andes, or the Alps, but the view from the top was spectacular. The entire Rhone Valley and its villages spread out before us as far as the eye could see. The villages below seemed no bigger than Lego towns. Roads crisscrossed the landscape like narrow ribbons of asphalt. Fields blanketed the earth like a patchwork quilt. From the mountaintop, we could take in the breadth of the land. Standing high above the everyday, it was easy to see the greatness of our God.

But God has not promised to give us a mountaintop view every day. Instead, He promised to give us a "lamp." (Psalm 119:105) In Old Testament times, this lamp would have been a simple bowl of oil with a wick. It would give you just enough light for a step or two down the path. God is so generous to us. He gives us just enough light to take the next step of obedience. He doesn't overwhelm us by sharing what He wants us to do tomorrow. He doesn't show us the challenges He will help us face next month. God gives us just enough light to obey Him today. We entrust the other 364 days of the year to His care. With the apostle Paul, we can say, "(For we walk by faith, not by sight:)" (2 Cor. 5:7).

Day after day, God lights one step at a time. In the daily walk of faith, God keeps us interested, engaged, and constantly surprised. We cannot see the next step around the corner. But we do know that it will be an adventure, and that God will walk with us. We learn to trust God and rely on His grace every single day. If we already knew what the rest of our day, year, or life held, we could fall into two different traps. Either we would panic at the scope and size of God's plans, or we would yawn and doze off for a nap. Neither of those options is best for our emotional or spiritual health. By giving us enough light for today, God teaches us to trust Him.

For people like Moses, Peter, James, and John, God revealed Himself through unique mountaintop experiences. Throughout the pages of Scripture, there are a handful of mountaintop events in the lives of God's people. Millions of believers walked through the centuries which the Bible covers. Yet only a handful of them had a mountaintop experience that irreversibly changed them, the people around them, and the course of their nation. Church history bears witness to this truth as well. For every Martin Luther, there are millions of believers–like you and me–who never experience a dramatic mountaintop moment. Instead, a gentle light from the Lamp guides us daily. It opens our eyes to see the hand of Jesus in commonplace moments and teaches us to be thankful for God's loving work in our lives.

The truth is that the everyday is not a mountaintop, or a 400-metre sprint. In reality, life is a long pilgrimage. We could not live on the mountaintop every day, since it would be exhausting and unsustainable. Instead, God calls us to live every minute in the light of His Word. In the everyday, His light is sufficient to guide your decisions.

The People of the Everyday

In the everyday, we can seek to know God. Look to the right or left of your path, and you can catch a glimpse of His divine character. How does God reveal Himself through the everyday? First, nature itself demonstrates the power, wisdom, and creativity of God. Scripture tells us that, "The heavens declare the glory of God..." (Psalm 19:1)

But what about people? The book of Genesis tells us that mankind was created in the image and likeness of God (Genesis 1:26). We can learn as much about God from the men, women, and children that He created as we can learn from natural beauty. God has shown mankind His *glory* in creation and His *image* in humanity. Too often, we focus on the faults and weaknesses in the people God created. We don't take the time to stop and ask, "What strengths and virtues does this person have? How do they reflect God's character and glory?"

Often, we as believers mistakenly think that we are the only ones who bear the image of God. But this idea is based on faulty reasoning. We must acknowledge the truth of James 1:17, "Every good gift and every perfect gift is from above, and cometh down from the Father of lights..." Any good thing–in anyone–is a gift from God. God has planted that good thing–a reflection of His image–in their hearts when He created them.

Almost everyone has a general goodwill for their fellow men. Even those who claim no religion show kindness and generosity to those in need. Everyday heroes risk their lives to save another's life. Military personnel serve their nations with no regard for personal security. Strangers step in to provide first aid at the scene of tragic accidents. Mothers and fathers devote years to raising their children with loving concern, generosity, and great personal sacrifice. In all these cases, people reflect the goodness and grace of their Creator.

Why does God create virtue in sinful people? He uses them to reveal aspects of His character to others. They also teach people to recognize the good in others and in God Himself. For example, if no one had ever shown you a paper dollar, would you recognize its worth when you found one blowing down the street? Likely, you would not. However, not everything we do reflects the image of God. Often, our life displays selfishness or traits of our "father the devil..." (John 8:44) But, enough of God's original image shines through to point man to Him.

Kindness, generosity, courage, strength, service, altruism, and so many other virtues we see in everyday life are all tiny snapshots of the character of our God. Keep your eyes open to see His reflection in the man on the street, the child next door, and the teen in your Sunday School class.
In what other ways can we seek God in the everyday? Let's explore the work, the challenges, and the triumphs of the everyday.

The Work of the Everyday

Most of us wish that we could live on permanent vacation. We think that a life of ease and luxury would be ideal. After all, we could develop our own interests without the pressures of a job, mortgage, and car payment. But God hasn't wired us for continual leisure. God is a worker! He laboured for six days to create the universe and rested on the seventh. He planned our salvation from the beginning of time and continues to carry out His plan through the centuries. He has guided, provided for, and blessed the nation of Israel. And He continues to work on behalf of His chosen people. His hand holds the very building blocks of the universe together. Colossians 1:17 tells us, "And he is before all things, and by him all things consist." When we work, we display the character of a God who works diligently on both a global and a personal level.

How does God's example of work impact our lives? The reality of God as a Worker should transform our view of work. Work is not a curse to be avoided or a heavy burden to carry. Proverbs 14:23a teaches us, "In all labour there is profit..." What profit do we gain from work? We gain skills, knowledge, and strength. We develop endurance and maturity. Work gives us a sense of accomplishment and provides many tangible rewards. We may be rewarded with delicious food on our table, a healthy savings account, and nice possessions. Or we may have intangible rewards—the thanks of a tired mother we helped, the satisfaction of finishing a difficult task, or watching the growth of young believers we counselled. God created us to work.

When Jesus lived among us, He worked. In John 5:19-20, Jesus told His disciples,

> ...Verily, verily, I say unto you, The Son can do nothing of himself, but what he seeth the Father do: for what things soever he doeth, these also doeth the Son likewise. For the Father loveth the Son, and sheweth him all things that himself doeth: and he will shew him greater works than these, that ye may marvel.

God the Father modelled work for His Son. Jesus saw the works of His Father and did the same works—healing, teaching, and doing good. Likewise, we should imitate Jesus' model of work. For the first thirty years of His life, Jesus lived an ordinary life. He likely cut wood, drew water, and carried out routine tasks. Apprenticing with his earthly father Joseph, He laboured as a humble carpenter. His hands bore calluses, and His body knew fatigue just like any man. Do you think He ever complained or became impatient with the timetable of God? Did He ever long for an escape from day after day of backbreaking toil? I don't think Jesus complained about the work God had given Him to accomplish. In Matthew 20:28, He said, "Even as the Son of man came not to be ministered unto, but to minister, and to give his life a ransom for many." Jesus was here to serve. Are you?

Christians should be the best workers on the job, in the classroom, and in the home. Remember this verse? "Whether therefore ye eat, or drink, or whatsoever ye do, do all to the glory of God." (1 Corinthians 10:31) As Christians, we should be the ones who show up early, stay cheerful under pressure, and maintain a standard of excellence. We should maintain a thankful attitude and work earnestly, "...as to the Lord, and not unto men; Knowing that of the Lord ye shall receive the reward of the inheritance: for ye serve the Lord Christ." (Colossians 3:23-24) Like Jesus, we ought to, "Do all things without murmurings and disputings: That ye may be blameless and harmless, the sons of God, without rebuke, in the midst of a crooked and perverse nation, among whom ye shine as lights in the world." (Philippians 2:14-15) What reputation do you have at work? Are you seeking to serve God in your everyday work?

The Challenges of the Everyday

With the work of the everyday, God also gives us everyday challenges. We encounter stress we can't handle, needs we can't meet, and people we can't seem to please. Life spills a tall glass of milk on our perfectly scripted plans, and we have to grab the paper towel and regroup. These everyday challenges force us to seek God.

Ask yourself the question, "Does God have any challenges in his daily work?" Actually, God does face challenges every day. The devil and his demons are still attempting to overthrow Him and take the throne of the universe. Knowing that his time is short, the devil destroys anything good that he can. He does his best to prevent people from believing on Christ, and He works to discourage Christians. His demons spread lies and false doctrine far and wide.

Besides them, we create daily challenges for God. We refuse to listen to His voice, ignore His Word, and rebel against His will. Thinking we know better than He does, we rush in where angels fear to tread. We neglect to seek Him. Instead, we rely on our own resources, but we are dumbfounded when we come to the end of our rope. We indulge in sin, limiting our usefulness for the Kingdom. We limit the work of God with our unbelief. Our sin and self-will are an everyday challenge for God.

What is God's goal for our lives? He's working to make us reflect more of Jesus and less of ourselves. He's accomplishing the intent of creation. The Bible tells us that, at salvation, we become "a new creature" in Jesus Christ. (2 Corinthians 5:17) God's intent for our character hasn't changed. From His creation of the first Adam, God intended for humanity to reflect His image. Though His plan was delayed by the fall of man in the Garden, He has now renewed this plan in the Second Adam, Jesus. Believers in Christ are a new creation, with new hearts and a new Spirit in their hearts. Through the process of sanctification, God changes us to reflect His Image.

Like us, God faces everyday challenges. The devil, his demons, and even we make God's work in this world more challenging. Yet He exhibits great patience. "It is of the Lord's mercies that we are not consumed, because his compassions fail not." (Lamentations 3:22) God handles His challenges with love, grace, and patience. He gives us mercy balanced with justice. He acts within the framework of eternal truth. God is never worried or anxious about the results. He has perfect peace in the midst of challenges.

As we encounter everyday challenges, we must follow God's perfect example of handling challenges. Watching His compassion, grace, and kindness, we learn how to handle the challenges of people. We can study how He balances truth with love, and mercy with justice. The mercy God has shown to us challenges us to pass on mercy to others. We can imitate God's model by handling challenges with grace, wisdom, and truth. Everyday challenges open the door for us to seek God fervently—both for His example and His strength.

The Triumphs of the Everyday

As we seek God in the everyday, we also see His hand in our triumphs. In everyday triumphs, we learn the depth of God's love, grace, and generosity. However, we don't hit a home run every day. Before every major victory comes thousands of tiny victories.

For example, one of Michelangelo's most famous works was the ceiling of the Sistine Chapel. As the story goes, one of his rivals, Bramante, persuaded the pope to commission Michelangelo in an unfamiliar medium(paint), so that he would fail. Michelangelo laboured for four years to complete the ceiling. Suspended on staging high above the ground, his muscles ached, and his eyes burned from paint dripping into them. Michelangelo depicted the Creation, the Fall of Man, prophecy, and the genealogy of Christ. His scenes sparkle with grace, elegance, and light. His composition, balance, and use of light are unmatched. During those four years, Michelangelo had many small triumphs. One by one, he crafted characters from Biblical and classical history. I think he gave thanks for every scene completed and every square foot of vivid colour. Had he given up too soon, the world would never have the cultural treasure that is the ceiling of the Sistine Chapel. Like Michelangelo, we should give thanks for every victory, no matter how ordinary. God uses small victories to encourage our hearts.

What daily victories do we experience? Most of us are not Michelangelo, Dickens, or the apostle Paul. But we can be thankful for every little gift from God. Perhaps little Susanna finally learns to ride a bike without training wheels—at least for a hundred feet, before she crashes it in the grass. Or, you find the exact brand of candy that you've been looking for. Maybe you prayed for chicken to go on sale this week, and, when you open the flyers, chicken is at the top of the front page! What about the little victory of being able to pay *something* on that unexpected bill? Or, after months of working on reading with little Mark, he finally catches on and exclaims, "I like reading!" Perhaps your pastor preaches on your absolutely favourite verse at prayer meeting. Or your next-door neighbour comes over with an armful of extra rhubarb from her patch. God loves to give us little silver boxes of blessing.

Sometimes, if we look closely enough, we can also see God's sense of humor. He knows exactly what will make us laugh. I think that the sound of God's children laughing(at funny things, not anything questionable) makes Him happy. He helps us laugh about our silly blunders, about the irony of life, and about the minor catastrophes of everyday life. Laughter does us good like a medicine (Proverbs 17:22). It relieves stress and gives us a balanced perspective. If we don't take ourselves too seriously, we can have a lot of fun.

The triumphs of the everyday are not merely good gifts that God gives us. They are so much more. If we seek God in the everyday, we can see and know Him. Everyday triumphs are snapshots that reveal the character of God to us. Those small moments are transformative time capsules that a Kodak print could never capture or contain. Do you cherish the moments of triumph where you saw Jesus?

What about the triumphs of averted disasters? Perhaps you accidentally stepped out in front of an oncoming car or a railroad track—only to be alerted to your danger by the blast of a horn or the scream of the oncoming locomotive's whistle. Maybe you found a puppy whimpering in your yard and returned it to her owner. What about the four-year-old child that you grabbed just before he fell off the porch? These events could have been bad—very bad—for you and for others. Often, the triumph of today was the disaster that God prevented.

In a moment of grace, God stepped into your day in a visible way. Don't dismiss it. Seek to see His love and care in the everyday. Recognize how He uses you to serve others. Give thanks when He uses people to save you from pain. So often, we blame God when things go wrong. But we don't thank Him when He steps in and saves the day. God works in our lives through small and great triumphs. When He steps in, seek Him with a heart of gratitude.

> *From Claudine*
>
> *I love how God gives us moments to laugh together and share His sense of humor! One of my favourite funny stories happened at my mom's Christian drama club. At this club, children and teens act out Bible stories and develop acting skills. One day, we improvised the story of the Fall of Man. I was assigned to play Eve, and a four-year-old boy named Jack was given the role of Adam. It went pretty smoothly until that pivotal moment when I offered Jack an imaginary fruit. "Here," I said in my sweetest, most persuasive tones, "Try it. It's really good!" Jack stepped backward with a determined frown on his little face. Raising his hands defensively, he declared, "No! I won't take it!" He flatly refused to accept the fruit. Jack knew where this story was going, and he wasn't going to mess it up for the rest of humanity! We all enjoyed a good laugh about Jack's quick thinking. And I think God chuckled, too!*

Seeing His Hand in the Everyday

As we seek Jesus in the ordinary details of life, we can see His hand at work. We should not expect a mountaintop experience every day. Although mountaintop experiences are a blessing, they are rare. Instead, we should seek to walk in the light of His presence daily. Like the woman of Matthew 9, we should be satisfied to simply touch the hem of His garment. Like Elijah on Mount Horeb, we should listen for His still, small voice. If we seek Him in the everyday, we can learn much about Him.

How does God teach us about Himself through the everyday? In the ordinary faces of your family, your church, and your community, the image of God shines forth. Despite their imperfections, people can reflect God's goodness, generosity, and virtue. In the work of the everyday, Jesus is our model. Like His work on earth, our work can be meaningful, joyful, and profitable. In the challenges of the everyday, we recognize the grace of God toward us. We seek Him for strength and courage to conquer the giants in our life. In the triumphs of the everyday, we seek God. He leaves behind fingerprints of His goodness, His grace, and His protection in every triumph.

Will you seek God in the everyday? His presence is not limited to your devotional time or your church attendance. As Jesus said, "Abide in me, and I in you. As the branch cannot bear fruit of itself, except it abide in the vine; no more can ye, except ye abide in me." (John 15:4) Seeking God in the everyday means abiding in His presence and learning to walk with Him. There is no greater life and no deeper joy!

CHAPTER 11
Seeking God for Guidance

"The steps of a good man are ordered by the LORD:
and he delighteth in his way.
Though he fall, he shall not be utterly cast down:
for the LORD upholdeth him with his hand."
Psalm 37:23-24

As we seek God through the challenges and triumphs of the everyday, we face many decisions. Some decisions are trivial, such as our dinner menu or our weekend plans. Yet other decisions carry significant weight. What neighborhood should we live in? What church should we attend? Who should we choose for our closest friends? Decisions, both large and small, determine both the direction and the impact of our lives.

To make wise decisions, we should seek God for guidance and wisdom. We want His approval and blessing on our decisions. Often, we refer to the Scriptural concept of God's will when we talk about decisions. In truth, God's will includes two categories.

1) God's General Will
The Bible reveals God's general will for all people. He wants all to accept His gift of salvation (1 Timothy 2:4), do good works (Ephesians 2:10), live a holy life (1 Peter 1:15-16), and be thankful (1 Thessalonians 5:18). The Bible teaches many clear commands and principles of God. We can have no doubt that lying is sin, that we must honour our parents, or that we should share the gospel with the lost. These mandates are part of God's general will for His people.

2) God's Specific Will
As our loving Father, God has a specific will for each of us. His specific will includes decisions He has already made for our lives *and* decisions that He allows us to make. God chose the day of your birth, the family you would

enter, and the specific strengths and weaknesses you would possess. Each of us has been given a tailor-made set of gates to walk through, giants to defeat, and dilemmas to solve. God's will for your life may be radically different than His will for someone else's life. If we seek His guidance, we can thrive within His specific will for our lives.

In this chapter, we'll focus on God's specific will for our lives. How can we discover it? How can we seek His guidance to make wise decisions? Let's begin by considering the plans we make.

Man's Plans

Throughout Christian popular culture, we encounter many misconceptions about God's will. One key misconception is based on the fallacy of predeterminism. According to the Oxford Dictionary, predeterminism is, "the belief that all events, including human actions, are established or decided in advance." The Christianized version of this fallacy would be, "God has already decided all events, including human actions, before the foundation of the world." This concept would make God the author of sin, evil, and countless atrocities. It would rob us of the power to choose, a critical aspect of the divine Image.

Predeterminism implies that man has no legitimate free will. If we believe it, this fallacy removes our responsibility to make wise decisions. It makes our choices meaningless. If each choice has been already made by God, why should I seek His direction? Why should I ask for wise counsel? This fallacy even provides an excuse for sin. After all, if someone else sinned, God must have planned it. Why can't I sin, too?

However, the Bible does not teach the concept of predeterminism. God allowed Adam and Eve to choose the forbidden fruit. In Joshua 24:15, the Israelite people had to choose, "And if it seem evil unto you to serve the Lord, choose you this day whom ye will serve..." Jesus said, "...If any man *will* come after me, let him deny himself, and take up his cross, and follow me." (Matthew 16:24, emphasis added) Jesus invites us to respond to Him, "Behold, I stand at the door, and knock: if any man hear my voice, and open the door, I will come in to him, and will sup with him, and he with me." (Revelation 3:20)

In truth, God gives us countless decisions to make as we see fit. Consider the relationship between a parent and child. As a toddler, the child only makes short-term, inconsequential decisions. *What kind of ice cream would you like? Which book would you like to read?* As the child grows in knowledge and character, the parent offers more decisions. The child learns to make more significant decisions. *What should you include in your budget? What kind of friends do you want to have? Are your friends helping you grow spiritually?* Parents can still veto harmful decisions. But, when parents allow a few shortsighted decisions, the child learns to analyze them and choose more wisely in future. In a similar way, God equips us to make wise decisions. As we grow spiritually, He gives us more complex and extensive decisions to make. Mature believers know how to make wise decisions within God's specific will for their lives.

As a case in point, consider Jesus' parable of the talents in Matthew 25. Jesus told His disciples,

> For the kingdom of heaven is as a man travelling into a far country, who called his own servants, and delivered unto them his goods. And unto one he gave five talents, to another two, and to another one; to every man according to his several ability; and straightway took his journey. (Matt. 25:14-15)

During their master's absence, two of the servants invested their talents. Because of their diligence, they reaped double the money they had invested. The third servant was lazy, so he buried his talent in the ground. After a long time, the master returned from his journey. He summoned his three servants and asked for a report. When the first two servants reported their gains, he praised them and rewarded them with more responsibility. When the lazy servant plodded up to the throne, he offered a pathetic excuse for his lack of gain. His master rebuked him harshly, "Thou wicked and slothful servant, thou knewest that I reap where I sowed not, and gather where I have not strawed: Thou oughtest therefore to have put my money to the exchangers, and then at my coming I should have received mine own with usury." (Matt. 25:26-27) Because of his laziness and rebellion, the wicked servant lost his one talent, and he was cast into outer darkness.

In this fascinating parable, the master (who represents God) did not supervise his servants. He did not provide appointments with a stock broker, a stack of books on investing, or a list of the best mutual funds. He had already given them ability, wisdom, and talents to invest. Now the responsibility for action rested on their shoulders. How would they invest their talents? In the end, the master praised the servants who invested wisely and reaped rewards. He condemned the servant whose laziness trapped him in a cardboard box of excuses. Within God's specific will, He gives us many decisions. We are responsible to seek His guidance and choose wisely.

God's Plans

Since the beginning of human history, the plans of God have intersected with the plans of man. As we noted in chapter 1, God sought Abraham, Isaac, and Jacob to found the Israelite nation. For Israel's sake, God rebuked enemy nations, parted the Jordan River, and performed many miracles. As long as Israel sought Him, God clearly guided her steps and blessed her richly. When the fullness of time had come, God sent His only Son into the world. The promised Messiah fulfilled His Father's plans to the letter. Christ came, "To give knowledge of salvation unto his people by the remission of their sins, Through the tender mercy of our God; whereby the dayspring from on high hath visited us, To give light to them that sit in darkness and in the shadow of death, to guide our feet into the way of peace." (Luke 11:77-79) He died on an old rugged cross, was buried, and rose on the third day. Because of His sacrifice, salvation was offered to all who would believe on Him.

After Christ's ascension to heaven, God sent the Holy Spirit to indwell the apostles and new converts. He revealed to the apostles that salvation was for all nations, not only Israel. In the early years of Christianity, the gospel took hold in Asia Minor. It also blossomed in northern Africa. God sent Paul to Macedonia, Greece, to spread the gospel westward. In Europe, the gospel flourished. The Bible was translated into its many languages and strongly influenced the growth of Western civilization.

In 1455, Johannes Gutenberg printed the English Bible with a groundbreaking printing press. From approximately 1517-1648, the Protestant Reformation revolutionized Europe. Men like Martin Luther, Ulrich Zwingli, and John Calvin rebuked the corruption and heresy in the Church. They called for reforms and a return to the purity of the gospel. New churches sprang up and flourished despite severe persecution. In the 1700s, God sparked extensive revivals in Scotland, England, and North America. Jonathan Edwards, George Whitefield, and the Wesley brothers challenged Christians to greater holiness, zeal, and faithfulness in prayer. God worked powerfully through these revivals, and countless thousands were converted.

In the early to mid-1700s, only a handful of Pietist and Moravian missionaries served in Asia. In 1784, English Baptists and other non-conformists began to pray for a global revival. God heard their prayers. Near the end of the century, He called a man named William Carey into missions. Carey's motto was, "Expect great things from God. Attempt great things for God." Carey spread his vision for missions with his fellow Englishmen. After one of his compelling speeches in 1792, the Northamptonshire Baptist Association decided to found a missionary society. In 1793, William sailed for India with his family. There, he laboured in evangelism, discipleship, and translation of the Bible into the native languages. Following in his footsteps, tens of thousands of missionaries have gone around the world to spread the gospel of Jesus Christ.

These examples are only a small snapshot of how God has worked throughout history. To carry out His plans, God called individuals to pursue specific careers, or marry specific spouses, or live in specific places. His goal was the advance of His kingdom. Today, God has plans that extend far beyond our lives. These overarching plans may clash with ours. If this happens, we must be ready to accept His plans.

We must not assume that God has only one right option for every major decision. Too often, we view life as a complex math exam, with only one set of correct answers. We are paralyzed with the fear of choosing the wrong option. However, if God's plans do not cross ours, He gives us the freedom to choose. There may be several jobs in which we could succeed, several people with whom we could have a happy marriage, or several ministries where He could use us. God's will is not so rigid and inflexible that it will shatter into a million pieces if we make the wrong decision.

Under the New Covenant, we as believers have the Holy Spirit living in our hearts. We have the privilege of His counsel and direction. Outside the constraints of time, God can see far better than us what the best choices would be. "A man's heart deviseth his way: but the Lord directeth his steps." Proverbs 16:9 If we are seeking Him, we do have freedom to make many decisions. God promises to direct our steps within the parameters of His will. We are so blessed to have the benefit of His wisdom and guidance.

How to Seek God for Guidance

How can we seek God for guidance? Here are six essential steps to knowing God's will.

1) Yield your dreams and desires to God.
Be honest with God about what you want. What are your deepest hopes, desires, and dreams? You may dream of travelling the world, starting your own business, or getting married and having a family. If you faced no limitations of time, resources, or geography, what would you do? You can be honest with God about your dreams. Tell Him even the ones you've never shared with a living soul and the ones that seem impossibly big. He already knows what they are! After you have named your dreams and desires, lay them down at the feet of Jesus. Ask Him to give you His dreams instead.

Psalm 37:4 promises, "Delight thyself also in the Lord: and he shall give thee the desires of thine heart." If we are seeking God, He will change our desires to match His dreams for our life. We will begin to love what He loves and want what He wants. Sometimes, God gives us dreams so that He can fulfill them more perfectly than we could ever imagine. Trust that His dreams for you are far better than your own. "For the Lord God is a sun and shield: the Lord will give grace and glory: no good thing will he withhold from them that walk uprightly." (Psalm 84:11)

2) Be obedient today.
What has God already directed you to do? Ask yourself, "Has God told me to do something which I have not done? Have I ignored His clear direction in my life?" Pause right now, and ask God this question with an open heart. Be willing to obey Him. If God reveals something you need to do, respond. Ask His forgiveness for not obeying the first time, and commit to promptly obey Him now. *When you get serious with God, He'll get serious with you.* If you are obeying God today, you can trust that He will guide you for tomorrow.

3) Study the Word for principles and examples.
Though the Bible may not specifically address your situation, you should search for general principles to guide you. Some principles are always applicable, such as love for God, love for others, and holiness. Also, peruse the Bible for examples of people in your situation. How did Isaac find a wife? How did God call Paul into the ministry? How did Ruth meet Boaz? How did Abraham respond to God's test of faith?

4) Pray much for God's guidance.
Every day, ask for His wisdom and direction. God commands us in James 1:5, "If any of you lack wisdom, let him ask of God, that giveth to all men liberally, and upbraideth not; and it shall be given him." God has vast reserves of wisdom available for all who ask.

Learn to wait on God in prayer. In your quiet time, ask God specific questions. "What do you want me to do about this? When should I do this?" The Holy Spirit may speak to your heart in a still, small voice. His words will always be in agreement with Scripture. He will speak clearly and cohesively, and He will glorify Jesus. In John 16:13-14, Jesus said, "Howbeit when he, the Spirit of truth, is come, he will guide you into all truth: for he shall not speak of himself; but whatsoever he shall hear, that shall he speak: and he will shew you things to come. He shall glorify me: for he shall receive of mine, and shall shew it unto you." The Holy Spirit reminds us of Jesus' words and guides us in obeying His will.

5) Seek wise counsel.
God can use godly, experienced Christians to give us wise counsel. Remember the example of the young King Rehoboam. Instead of listening to his father's wise counsellors, he followed the appealing advice of his peers. Because of this foolish choice, he lost much of his kingdom and narrowly avoided losing his throne. Because most of our peers have a level of knowledge comparable to our own, they may not be the best people to ask for advice. Instead, ask the men and women who have served God faithfully for a lifetime. Job 12:12 tells us, "With the ancient is wisdom; and in length of days understanding." We can gain invaluable wisdom from our elders.

6) Be alert to circumstances arranged by God.
Circumstances alone are not a sufficient guide for our decisions. However, God can use circumstances to confirm His will and fill in the details. He works through the details of people, resources, time, and opportunities. In Revelation 3:7-8, Jesus described Himself as, "he that openeth, and no man shutteth; and shutteth, and no man openeth..." He said, "I know thy works: behold, I have set before thee an open door, and no man can shut it..." If God has clearly shut a door in your life, don't stand there and stubbornly bang on it. Instead, step back, and look for an open door. Seek to see God's hand in the specific circumstances of your life.

Investing Our Talents

God also guides us through the innate aptitudes and talents He has given us. Perhaps you have a gift for teaching people, counselling, or conflict resolution. Some people have natural aptitudes for design, analysis, and the sciences. You may have a keen ear for music, a deft hand in the kitchen, or an artistic eye for photography. Take a moment to ask yourself what talents God has given you to invest. When God created you with these talents, He had a clear vision for how you could invest them. In 1 Timothy 4:14, Paul wrote to Timothy, " Neglect not the gift that is in thee, which was given thee by prophecy, with the laying on of the hands of the presbytery." In context, "the gift" refers to Timothy's spiritual gift. However, I think we can infer that we should not neglect our natural gifts either.

God did not call you to lock your gifts into a dusty trunk and throw the key away. He did not call you to hold back in fear of intimidating others. He did not call you to compare your gifts to those of others. Instead, God calls you to invest your gifts--without reservation or fear, joyfully embracing His vision for your life. "And whatsoever ye do, do it heartily, as to the Lord, and not unto men; Knowing that of the Lord ye shall receive the reward of the inheritance: for ye serve the Lord Christ." (Colossians 3:23-24) If you seek His guidance, He will help you invest your talents wisely and fruitfully.

Guidance for Our Ministry

If you want to serve God, cultivate a heart for ministry. Every day, ask God to use you and give you open doors. Ask for opportunities to share the gospel. Ask for people to serve. Keep your eyes open for needs to meet and people to encourage. Invest your talents, and learn skills to use in God's work.

God has already commanded us to go into all the world to preach the gospel. He has called us to give, to pray, and to make disciples. Don't be afraid to step out in faith to serve Him. What is the worst thing that could happen? You might step out into the wrong ministry at the wrong time. In that case, trust that God will redirect you into the right ministry. Always surround your efforts with prayer. Remember William's Carey's motto, "Expect great things from God. Attempt great things for God."

When God calls you into a ministry, you may not be able to see anything beyond your next step. His plans may seem impossibly big, difficult, or risky. Take the first step, and He will give you enough light for the next...and the next. "Have not I commanded thee? Be strong and of a good courage; be not afraid, neither be thou dismayed: for the Lord thy God is with thee whithersoever thou goest." (Joshua 1:9) As we seek God, we can be secure in His guidance and constant presence.

The Script of Our Life

When we think about the future, we often imagine what we would like. Perhaps you picture yourself stepping out of a shiny Chevy Camaro onto a smooth asphalt driveway. You stroll through a well-manicured garden and up the steps of a Colonial homestead. The maid opens the front door and offers you a tray of hors d'oeuvres. Inside, your spouse hands you tickets to watch your favourite sports team on the weekend. Your three perfectly behaved children are finishing their homework. Then you wake up, switch on the lamp, and realize it was a dream.

Sometimes, we write a detailed script for the future—complete with characters, setting, and plot. Then we hold it out to God, saying, "This is what I want to do. Will you please sign Your Name here at the bottom?" However, doing this forces God into a box of our expectations. And He doesn't fit into a box. God's ways are higher than our ways, and His thoughts infinitely higher than our thoughts. (Isaiah 55:9) He views our lives from His eternal, wise, omniscient perspective. If we insist on writing our own script, we will be disappointed when God does not follow it. His script for our lives may be a little different than what we imagined.

Instead of writing our own script and asking for God's signature, we should give Him a blank manuscript. At the bottom of every page, we should sign our name in bold, flowing letters. Our prayer should be, "My life is Yours, Lord. I know Your script is far better than anything I could write. Every moment, every hour—help me perform the role You have given me. Guide my decisions with Your wisdom." When we seek God's guidance and yield our future to Him, we will be richly blessed.

"For since the beginning of the world men have not heard, nor perceived by the ear, neither hath the eye seen, O God, beside thee, what he hath prepared for him that waiteth for him." (Isaiah 64:4)

CHAPTER 12

Seeking Him Through Discipline

*In reading the lives of great men,
I found that the first victory they won was over themselves...
self-discipline with all of them came first.
-Harry S. Truman*

Seeking Jesus is not a leisurely stroll in the park. If true Christianity was easy, more people would follow Jesus. But it's not effortless or easy. Walking with Jesus requires self-discipline. Discipline calls us to obey God regardless of our situation. It calls us to early morning devotions or midnight prayers for a loved one. It calls us to be faithful in attending, giving, and serving in our local church. As much as we hesitate to admit it, most of us need to develop our self-discipline.

Why is discipline crucial in our lives? God has a rewarding plan for your life and mine. He wants us to display the character of Jesus Christ. In fact, He will continue to work on us "until Christ be formed in you..." (Galatians 4:19) God will mold the clay of our character into a vessel of beauty and honour. He will teach us to put off the old man and put on the new man. (Ephesians 4:22-24) God has given us the mind of Christ (1 Cor. 2:16), and He will renew our thinking with His Word (Ephesians 4:23). The process of spiritual growth can be challenging and even uncomfortable. It demands that we have discipline.

In Mark 8:34, Jesus called us to self-discipline. He said, "Whosoever will come after me, let him deny himself, and take up his cross, and follow me." (Mark 8:34) The cross is a compelling symbol of self-discipline. For Jesus, His cross was His earthly mission. At the cross, He suffered to carry out the eternal plan of God for His years on earth. There, He acted nobly for the good of others, without trying to spare Himself pain and anguish. At the cross, He paid the ultimate price to redeem humanity.

Our cross should be no different. For us, the cross should be the place where we serve God and others unselfishly. Taking up the cross means accepting suffering as part of God's specific plan for your life. What does the discipline of the cross look like in everyday life?

1) Taking up our cross is about following–not about leading the way.
Many people have bought into an individualistic belief that they are in charge of their own lives. "All our dreams can come true, if we have the courage to pursue them," said Walt Disney. This belief is nothing new. Since the Garden of the Eden, the devil refused to heed God's voice. He didn't want anyone telling him what to do. Ever since, he's convinced people to join his rebellion against God.

As Christians, we know that God is in control–not us. He has a specific will for our life (see chapter 10), and we must submit to this will. Discipline is about *following* Jesus. It means adapting our lives to follow His teachings, His life, and His character.

2) Taking up our cross–of necessity–means laying down other things.
Let's be honest. We can't carry everything at once (though we try sometimes!) We can't carry all the worries, troubles, and even trophies (both our own and those of others) *and* carry our cross. We are only capable of carrying a certain amount. Perhaps we need to lay down tomorrow's cares and anxieties at His feet. Jesus Himself taught, "Take therefore no thought for the morrow: for the morrow shall take thought for the things of itself. Sufficient unto the day is the evil thereof." (Matthew 6:34) Also, we may need to leave yesterday's regrets in the closet. We cannot live in the past, reliving its victories and its defeats. Focusing on the past will prevent us from living today well. To take up the cross of discipline each day, we must recognize what is too heavy to carry and lay it down.

3) Taking up our cross means not worrying about what everyone else is carrying.
With our limited energy, time, and resources, we are only capable of carrying our own cross. In my experience, too many Christians are very concerned about how everyone else is living the Christian life. Unfortunately, they fail to effectively live their own life for Christ because they are too busy gossiping, blaming, and criticizing. If we are engrossed with drama in other people's lives, we will be distracted from carrying our own cross.

4) Taking up our cross – by definition – requires effort on our part.
The cross of Jesus was heavy – a burden. Carrying it required Him to expend energy and endure pain. Picking up your cross means choosing discipline over ease and self-centredness. However, let us state that a life

of unselfish service to God for the benefit of others is more rewarding than any other. It is a life of lasting joy, all-sufficient grace, and the abundant blessings of God. But it requires discipline.

In the New Testament, God gives us three examples of discipline. Let's take a look at them.

The Olympian

In 1 Corinthians 9:27, Paul tells us that the Olympian boxer brings his body "into subjection." He trains diligently to prepare for boxing. His self-discipline keeps him physically ready to compete. In 1 Timothy 4:7, Paul tells us to exercise ourselves unto godliness. Why does Paul use the metaphor of exercise? Life isn't a 400m sprint; it's a marathon. Eventually, you will come to the end of your enthusiasm, motivation, and willpower. At this critical point, your self-discipline will enable you to keep going and stay faithful to God.

In the physical realm, doctors refer to muscle memory. It is the ability to repeat a muscle movement that has been continually practiced. Both Olympians and other world-class athletes invest thousands of hours into their sport. They make extraordinary sacrifices and endure rigorous training. Athletes must be willing to push through pain, to tell their bodies to keep going, and to trust their coaches completely. They discipline themselves to do all these things.

Now, I'm no Olympian. I like *watching* the Olympics from the comfort of my La-Z-Boy™ chair. The closest I get to muscle memory is that my fingers know which keys to press on a keyboard without having to think too hard about it. However, the fact that I am not an athlete does not exempt me – or you – from the race of life. God has set before us a race, and it is our responsiblity to run it. In the marathon of life, discipline will enable us to keep running. We have to constantly practice the actions and decisions that we know are good for us. In time, they will become "muscle memory." Through discipline, we will learn to do right out of reflex.

The Soldier

Paul also used the metaphor of a soldier to describe the discipline necessary for the Christian life. He instructed Timothy to, "...endure hardness, as a good soldier of Jesus Christ." (2 Timothy 2:3)

Much like the Olympian, the soldier trains for thousands of hours for the one hour when he must perform perfectly. Soldiers don't walk into battle on their first day. They prepare with hour after hour of drills, mock battles, and workouts. Many Christians think that, when things get serious, they will be automatically be prepared to face trials, temptations, persecutions, and the attacks of the devil. In reality, preparation is necessary. If you don't put in the training every day by taking up your cross and following Christ, you won't be ready to walk with Him through the trials of this life. The soldier is only able to follow the general's orders because he has spent thousands of hours in training. If you want to endure and finish your course, you must discipline yourself daily.

The Farmer

Jesus taught us about the farmer. He said, "No man, having put his hand to the plough, and looking back, is fit for the kingdom of God." (Luke 9:62) He taught us how a farmer sows seed, waters it, and waits patiently for a harvest.

I may not be an Olympian. I'm certainly not a soldier. But I can relate to the farmer. The farmer takes a lot of money, buys seed, and plants it in the ground. He spends hours watering and fertilizing it. For weeks, he waits….and waits…and waits. The farmer invests countless hours of time, labour, and energy. Each day, he wakes up before dawn and goes to bed long after the sun has set. He carefully tends the fields – no matter what the weather.

Farming takes discipline – and a healthy dose of faith. The farmer must believe that the tiny seeds he planted will spring up, and that the crop will be good this year. Every day of hard work is one day closer to the harvest. At the core of a farmer's character is discipline.

We are called to be farmers. Jesus calls us to plant, to sow, to work tirelessly and diligently. But so many Christians are unwilling to pay the price to buy the seed. Much less will they do the daily work of planting, cultivating, fertilizing, and watering it.

Why are they so reluctant? Being a Christian takes discipline. It takes discipline to read your Bible each day, to study it, to memorize it, and to meditate on it. It takes discipline to cultivate a prayer life. It takes discipline to move beyond yourself to serve. You must have discipline to expend your time, talents, and treasure for the glory of God and the benefit of someone else. Both farming and faith require us to be disciplined before we can reap a harvest.

Taking Up Our Cross

As we seek Jesus, we must learn to take up the cross of discipline. The cross is the place where we forget ourselves in cheerful service to others. At the cross, we learn to obey God. We discipline ourselves to study the

Bible and conform our lives to its principles. We discipline ourselves to pray both in our private closets and in our spare moments, with our lips and in our heart of hearts.

At the cross, we bow to the will of our Father. At the cross, we endure suffering, misunderstanding, and persecution. Though the winds may blow violently and the rains beat upon our head, the cross of discipline enables us to endure.

The cross of discipline is often a heavy one. Sometimes, we may wonder if we will be able to carry this cross all the way Home. Our backs ache, and our feet grow weary. But, if we look just a little farther down the road, we will see Jesus, "...who for the joy that was set before him endured the cross, despising the shame, and is set down at the right hand of the throne of God." (Hebrews 12:2) If we take up the cross with Him, we will discover that His grace is enough to help us carry it all the way Home.

CHAPTER 13

The Joy of Seeking God

At the close of King David's reign, he calls a solemn assembly. The nation gathers to hear the last words of the elderly king. The mighty arms that felled enemies on every side have grown frail and weak. The hand that slung a stone to kill a giant now trembles slightly. The lips that shouted for a thousand victories speak softly now. A hush descends over the throngs, and David rises to speak.

> Hear me, my brethren, and my people: As for me, I had in mine heart to build an house of rest for the ark of the covenant of the Lord...But God said unto me, Thou shalt not build an house for my name, because thou hast been a man of war, and hast shed blood. Howbeit the Lord God of Israel chose me before all the house of my father to be king over Israel for ever...And he said unto me, Solomon thy son, he shall build my house and my courts: for I have chosen him to be my son, and I will be his father. Moreover I will establish his kingdom for ever, if he be constant to do my commandments and my judgments, as at this day. (1 Chronicles 28:2-4,6-7)

Although David longed to raise a temple, God did not permit him to build. Instead, God has appointed his son Solomon to raise a temple. Young and inexperienced, Solomon must now accept the solemn mantle of kingship. When he becomes king, his life will never be the same. Each word must be weighed and each step well-chosen. He will face enemies, rivals, and pressures from every side.

As King David steps down from the throne, he stands poised to give a parting word of wisdom. Perhaps he will advise him on political or military goals. He may give Solomon a hit list of Israel's most wanted criminals. Or he could describe the best way to find a wife. (Solomon certainly could have used that!) But David does not speak of politics, wealth, or marriage. Instead, he chooses something far wiser. David points his son to the One who has guided his every step, shielded him from wicked enemies, and placed a new song in his mouth. He charges Solomon:

> And thou, Solomon my son, know thou the God of thy father, and serve him with a perfect heart and with a willing mind: for the Lord searcheth all hearts, and understandeth all the imaginations of the thoughts: *if thou seek him, he will be found of thee;* but if thou forsake him, he will cast thee off for ever. (1 Chronicles 28:9, emphasis added)

At this pivotal moment, David speaks wisdom into Solomon's life. If the young king seeks God fervently, everything else will fall into place. If Solomon seeks the will of God, his steps will be directed. If he seeks the heart of God, his words will be wise and effective. If he seeks the hand of God, his life will be blessed beyond measure. If Solomon seeks the face of God, he will know life eternal and abundant joy.

Yet David cautions him, "...if thou forsake him, he will cast thee off for ever." If Solomon turns away from God, he will have freedom to live his own life. He can taste the sinful pleasures of the world, defy the law of God, and, for a time, escape judgment. But he will receive a tragic punishment. God will remove His blessing, His protection, and His presence from Solomon's life. As Solomon ascends the throne, he must chart a course for his life. Will he seek the Lord or forsake Him?

As a young king, Solomon chose to seek God wholeheartedly. And God richly blessed his life. Solomon became the wisest man on earth. From the east and the west, kings and queens visited him to hear his wisdom firsthand. King Solomon was renowned for his wealth, power, and glory. As long as Solomon sought God, he was incredibly blessed. And the favour of God rested on his life.

The Great Hall

Imagine with me for a moment a great hall set in the heart of a medieval castle. The vaulted ceiling stretches high above the tiled floor. Rich tapestries muffle every sound. Servants rush to and fro with rustic bread, game, and cheeses. You must enter through a narrow doorway. Stepping inside, you see table after table of people eating, talking, and laughing. At the far end of the hall, a raised dais holds the table of honour. Only the lord of the manor, his family, and his honored guests sit there. For a moment, you gaze respectfully towards the dais. Then, you look around for a seat with your friends. After all, you are just a commoner. You cannot expect to sit with the lord of the manor. He is practically unapproachable. Unless you get into extraordinary trouble, you will never attract his notice.

Salvation is like entering the great hall. To enter, we must believe on Jesus, the only Door. Inside the great hall, we are now in the same room as God Himself. Yet too many Christians stop at this point. They are happy with the blessings of the Christian life. They eat, talk, and laugh with everyone at the common tables. But they never lift their eyes to the dais, where the Lord sits. Though they have walked with God for five, ten, or forty years, they have never sat at the same table with Him. Many Christians haven't truly sought the presence of God. They haven't tasted the depth of relationship that He offers on this side of heaven.

Yet today the Lord of the manor invites you to approach His table. "Seek ye the Lord while he may be found, call ye upon him while he is near..." (Isaiah 55:6) He calls you to sit with Him, to enter His presence, and to taste His incredible goodness. Seeking Jesus means sitting at His table. It's pouring out your heart to Him, listening to His voice, and knowing His heart. It's precious and sweet. Once you sit down at His table, you will be hungry for more. Sitting at His table is the privilege of a lifetime.

One man who heard this illustration was deeply convicted. He came up to his pastor in tears and said something like this, "I've been saved for so many years, but I've never sat at that table. Once, I went up and asked for the ketchup. But I want to sit at that table." Jesus invites you to sit at His table. Will you come?

The Cost of Seeking God

To seek God, you must count the cost. The precious treasure of knowing God is not offered cheaply. Its cost is steep. God does not spill out His diamonds and emeralds before those who care nothing for jewels. Those who earnestly seek Him will be rewarded. Those who neglect Him will go on their merry way, never recognizing what glory they missed.

If we neglect to seek Him now, how great will be our regrets someday! To see Jesus and shrink as from a stranger—One we scarcely know—could this happen to us? Let us not fall into the trap of expecting Heaven to immediately give us a complete understanding of God. Heaven will be a learning and growing experience. We cannot ignore Him all our lives and wake up in Heaven with a more mature relationship with Jesus dropped into our lap. If we live outside His presence, we will deeply regret it. Relationships demand work and sacrifice.

But if you seek Him fervently now, you will truly enjoy Heaven. Your eyes will gaze on the One you have loved and longed for and sought fervently. Your heart will overflow with joy and rest! Your eyes will see the King in His beauty, and you will be satisfied. With Fanny Crosby, let us anticipate that moment.

When my lifework is ended, and I cross the swelling tide,
When the bright and glorious morning I shall see;
I shall know my Redeemer when I reach the other side,
And His smile will be the first to welcome me.

Oh, the soul-thrilling rapture when I view His blessed face,
And the luster of His kindly beaming eye;
How my full heart will praise Him for the mercy, love and grace,
That prepare for me a mansion in the sky.[1]

If we seek Him fervently, how glorious will be the day when we open our eyes in Heaven. Our eyes will gaze on our Beloved One, the One we have long sought for, glimpsed with eyes of faith, and embraced with arms of trust. He is the One who has walked with us through the clinging dust and weary toil of earth. How sweet it will be to step onto the other shore and find Him infinitely more beautiful than we ever imagined!

Seeking God will cost us time, love, and energy. He calls us to give up our rights and submit to His will. Can any sacrifice be too great for our precious Jesus? No! a thousand times! All sacrifices pale in the light of His radiance. Let us gladly fall at His worthy feet in sweet surrender. Let us purpose to seek Him no matter what the cost. Let us abandon every tie that would separate us from His presence. Let us rejoice in finding Him as one who finds great treasure. Every sacrifice will be richly rewarded. Like Isaiah, let us declare, "Here am I. Send me! All that I have, all that I am—it is Yours." For He promised, "And ye shall seek me, and find me, when ye shall search for me with all your heart." (Jeremiah 29:13)

Today, Jesus sets before us a choice. Will we seek Him as King Solomon did? Or will we forsake Him? This choice is not to be made lightly. We will only be as close to God as we want to be. He will not force us to seek Him. Yet, if we choose to forsake Him, we will reap a harvest of sorrow and separation, and regret. If we seek Jesus, we will find Him. Knowing Him will colour our lives with joy, freedom, and beauty. We will never regret a single moment we spend in loving, obeying, and seeking Jesus.

---

1. Selected lyrics from the hymn "My Saviour First of All." Crosby, Fanny.

FOR MORE BY JASON...

"HOMAN'S INSIGHTS ARE KEEN AND LUCID. THEY SHOULD BE READ AND EXAMINED BY PRAYERFUL HEARTS COMMITTED TO THE HISTORIC FAITH."

In *Before the Box*, Jason Homan takes us on a journey through the church describing the boxes (traditions, expectations, and extremes) in which modern Christianity has encased itself. To move forward in our spiritual lives and to make our churches most effective for Jesus, we must get back to a time before these traditions, expectations, and extremes, a time *Before the Box*.

What did these look like before the box?

- Motivation for Ministry
- Devotional Life
- World Evangelism
- Consistency and Balance
- Approach to Culture
- The Church
- Church Music
- Discipleship
- and more!
- Success
- Church Programs
- The Gospel
- Church Leadership Roles
- Good Works
- Separation
- Youth
- Innovation

DISCOVER WHAT CHRISTIANITY LOOKED LIKE...BEFORE THE BOX.

Available on Amazon in paperback and Kindle form.

FORWARD MARKETING

Forward Marketing Solutions is not primarily about social media, branding, websites, writing, and publishing.
We are about helping people succeed.
Your business, church, or non-profit has a message that you need to get out to the public...but you don't have time to do it yourself.
We can help.
We specialize in creating syndicated content (weekly blogs and social media graphics) for churches and businesses.
Let us be your outsourced online marketing department – creating and coordinating vibrant content and managing your online strategy.
Give us a call at (902) 304-4707! We'd be happy to talk.

"You've been a huge help in caring for our website blogs and social media. #soeasy!"
-Noah Sparkes, Northside Baptist Church

Forward takes care of everything for us! Ecommerce, website, social media, SEO...Thanks, team!
-Undercover Pet Houses

We also offer...

- Full Social Media Management
- Book and Print Design
- On Page SEO, Media Outreach
- Press Releases
- Google AdWords Campaigns
- Facebook Campaigns
- Remarketing
- Transcription Services,
- Explainer Videos
- Banner & Display Design
- Logo Design

LET US BE YOUR OUTSOURCED MARKETING DEPARTMENT.

www.forwardmarketing.ca

Made in the USA
Middletown, DE
23 July 2020